1955
VAH-7
Secret Navy Atom Bomber Squadron

COLD WAR WARRIOR TRILOGY

1955
VAH-7
Secret Navy Atom Bomber Squadron

David D. Ferman

Copyright © David D. Ferman.

All rights reserved. No part of this book may be reproduced in any form or by any electronic or mechanical means, including information storage and retrieval systems, without permission in writing from the publisher, except by reviewers, who may quote brief passages in a review.

ISBN: 978-1-64669-975-9   (Paperback Edition)
ISBN: 978-1-64669-976-6   (Hardcover Edition)
ISBN: 978-1-64669-974-2   (E-book Edition)

Every person that I wrote about in my Cold War Warrior Trilogy was, or hopefully still is a living woman or man. However, in my trilogy (*1953—Making A Marine Grunt Warrior, 1954—Making A Marine Pilot Warrior, 1955—VAH-7, Secret Navy Atom Bomber Squadron*), I changed the names of several persons in each book to avoid embarrassing them or their relatives. I owe those wonderful old rascals that much for being such good friends back then, and such great material for these three books now. Given all possible choices today, I would not and could not write these true stories in any other way.

These books are interesting, somewhat humorous and didactic because they are absolutely true. All of the events, places, attitudes and opinions are factual. It has been 64 years since 1955, so some other old duffer's memories may differ from mine.

Book Ordering Information

Phone Number: 347-901-4929 or 347-901-4920
Email: info@globalsummithouse.com
Global Summit House
www.globalsummithouse.com

Printed in the United States of America

TABLE OF CONTENTS

I. INTRODUCTION

1. SEA STORIES 1
2. BACKSTORY 2
   2.1 1953: MAKING A MARINE GRUNT WARRIOR 2
   2.2. 1954: MAKING A MARINE PILOT WARRIOR 7
   2.3. THE DAY I CRASHED, BURNED, AND NEARLY DROWNED. 10
   2.4. YOU SCRATCH MY BACK AND I'LL SCRATCH YOURS 18
   2.5. AN OFFER I COULD NOT REFUSE 20

II. THE U.S. NAVY'S GENERAL LEMAY PROBLEM

1. PLAN "A" 23
2. PLAN "B" 24
3. PLAN "C" 25

III. METAMORPHOSIS OF A COVERT APPRENTICE

1. NAS PATUXENT RIVER WAS SOFTBALL HEAVEN. 26
2. AIR INTELLIGENCE ALA FIRE HOSE 30
3. BIG BAD BOMB CHECKOFF LIST 31
4. BE IT EVER SO HUMBLE. 33
5. SNARKY PERSONNEL POGUE'S SILLY GAMES BACKFIRE. 35

IV. VAH-7 AT THE POINT OF THE SPEAR

1. ESCARGOT ALA BANG, BANG KABOOM 37
2. RABAT'S KASBAH AFTER DARK 40
3. AJ-2 SAVAGE ATOM BOMBER REDUX 41
4. VAH-7 DIRTY LITTLE SECRET 42
5. MEDITERRANEAN MUSTACHE MYSTIQUE 44
6. SCURVY A'PLENTY IN 1955 45
7. HAPPINESS IS A PUSHCART FULL OF CHERRY BOMB FIRECRACKERS. 46
8. CUTE CAIO BELLA STOWAWAY AT SEA 47
9. TOP SECRET INFORMATION; NOT FUN AND GAMES 48
10. SALTY OLD CHIEF BOSUN MATE'S GAFF 50
11. "UNTIL THE REAL THING COMES ALONG, CHA, CHA, CHA." 51
12. PHOTO BANSHEE HOT SHOTS 53
13. HOLY HAL'S COMEUPPANCE. 56
14. NASTY GENOA WATERFRONT NEIGHBORHOOD 57
15. THE ROCK OF GIBRALTAR 62
16. A FINE DAY IN PALERMO, SICILY. 64
17. CLARE BOOTHE LUCE ALMOST VISITS US AT SEA. 66
18. OUR TOUR GUIDE WORE TWO HATS 68
19. AWOL ALL DAY IN SUNNY BARCELONA, SPAIN 68

20. NAVY STYLE DISCIPLINE 70
21. NAVY/MARINE "E" FOR EXCELLENCE AWARD 71
23. LAMBORGHINI TAXI CAB'S RACE 73
23. CHEAP EXTRACURRICULAR FIRE INSURANCE 74
24. PROMOTION BY DEFAULT 76
25. ATHENS' ACROPOLIS AFTER DARK 78
26. WITH FRIENDS LIKE THESE, WHO NEEDS ENEMIES? 79
27. READY ROOM "TALKER" BY DEFAULT 80
28. FARMER DAVE (SAY WHAT?) 81
29. ROME HAS MANY ATTRACTIONS. 82
30. KEEN COMPETITION—THE LOSERS WON 83
31. BEIRUT — "THE PARIS OF THE MEDITERRANEAN" 85
32. THE "WILD WEST" OF THE MIDDLE EAST 92
33. AIR JORDAN FLIES LOWER. 94
34. YOUNG MO SPEAKS MANY LANGUAGES A LITTLE BIT 97
35. 40MM TARGET PRACTICE ON THE DEAD SEA 106
36. THE ISRAELI ARMY'S "MAD MOMENT" 110
37. MISSION PROBABLY ACCOMPLISHED, OR NOT 113
38. USS CORAL SEA'S RESIDENT SMART GUY 120
39. AJ-2 MISSION IMPROBABLE 121
40. STRESS IS A BOOGER BEAR. 124
41. WORLD WAR III BEGINS AT SEA? 125
42. ISTANBUL'S EXOTIC LITTLE SHEBA'S SEVENTH VEIL 127
43. "YANKEES GO HOME" IN BODY BAGS. 128
44. OLD ACQUAINTANCES NOT FORGOTTEN 133
45. FORCE 10 (?) STORM AT SEA 137
46. AJ-2 BOMBER'S TROUBLED TACTICS 141
47. CHEAP BERETTA PISTOL 145
48. THE BIG FLOATER: A 24/7 CARD GAME 146
49. PAY DAY HEIST 148
50. U.S. MARINE QUOTE 149

V. GOING HOME THE HARD WAY

1. THE AJ-2 FACTOR 150
2. BROKEN ARROW 151
3. CLASSIFIED JUNK 153
4. MAGNIFICENT ITALIAN CARAVAN 154
5. 21 DECEMBER 1955 155
6. 22 DECEMBER 1955 157
7. 23 DECEMBER 1955 158
8. 24 DECEMBER 1955 160
9. 25 DECEMBER 1955 162
10. ADMIRAL OFSTIE'S GOLD-PLATED TRAVEL ORDERS 162
11. LT. MILLSAP DOMINOED. 163
12. SAVING ME FROM MYSELF. 165
13. AJ-2 CRASHED IN THE SANFORD CITY DUMP. 167
14. DOOMS DAY ALARM 169
15. "ADIOS" ITCHY SOUP STRAINER 171
16. SAYONARA SQUADRON VAH-7. 171

VI. IN MEMORIUM

IN MEMORIUM 173

LIST OF FIGURES

Figure 1. Recruit Platoon 118, Day 3 in Boot Camp 3
Figure 2. The Author Played Semi-Pro Baseball to Earn Contracts from the Boston Red Sox 4
Figure 3. Drill Instructors' School Graduation 5
Figure 4. Recruits Firing at the 500-Yard Line at Camp Mathews 6
Figure 5. Marine Trained Rat..6
Figure 6. Navy SNJ Texan Fighter Training Aircraft.......................8
Figure 7. USAF T-34 Mentor Trainer Aircraft 8
Figure 8. Confederate Air Corps Induction 9
Figure 9. Author With SNJ 10
Figure 10. AJ-2 Savage Bomber 30
Figure 11. USS Lake Champlain CVA-39...38
Figure 12 Soviet MIG-15 Fighter Aircraft..42
Figure 13. F9F Fighter Aircraft..51
Figure 14. VF-11 Banshee Buzzing Anchored USS Lake Champlain 55
Figure 15. Acropolis of Athens-Original Porch of the Maidens 78
Figure 16. FJ-Fury Fighter Aircraft...84
Figure 17. Author and Friends Arriving in East Jerusalem 97
Figure 18: River Jordan Near Jerico..98
Figure 19. Street of the Chain..99

Figure 20. Damascus Gate 100
Figure 21. Walls of Biblical Jericho Emerge 103
Figure 22. Jordan River Basin 104
Figure 23. Boulders in Jordanian Wilderness 106
Figure 24. Shepherds and Desolation 107
Figure 25. More Jordanian Desert 108
Figure 26. More Jordanian Wilderness 108
Figure 27. Nativity Church in Bethlehem 111
Figure 28. Wailing Wall 114
Figure 29. Way of the Cross 115
Figure 30. Golgotha 115
Figure 31. Garden of Gethsemane 116
Figure 32. Dome of the Rock 116
Figure 33. The Mount of Olives 116
Figure 34 Dome of the Rock from Mount of Olives 117
Figure 35 The Tomb of Kings 117
Figure 36. The Pools of Bathezda 117
Figure 37. Green Line in Jerusalem
    (Jordan in Foreground, Israel in Background,
    Green Line in Between) 118
Figure 38. Blue Mosque in Istanbul 134
Figure 39. AJ-2 Atom Bomber Up Close in Gun Tub 151
Figure 40. AJ-2 Atom Bomber, Distant in Gun Tub 152
Figure 41. 40 MM Gun Tub 152

I. INTRODUCTION

1. SEA STORIES

Many civilians and boot recruits may ask: "What the heck is a sea story?"

An ancient and honorable tradition among the sea-going military services, sea stories are the most popular, highly preferred method of passing worthwhile information among the many millions of active duty, reserve and retired sailors and Marines. Make no mistake about it, authentic sea stories are always true (no scuttlebutt allowed), often humorous, usually first-person yarns about unusual and/or wondrous adventures such as grand and glorious victories, close calls, embarrassing faux pas, stupid mistakes, terrifying moments, dastardly deeds, galling disappointments, exotic locations, bawdy entertainment, hijinks when hammered, the women of (pick a place), "Dear John" letters and their often unforeseen consequences, commendations, awards, that 10 percent that never gets the word, regrettable foul ups, interesting trivia, or anything else worth mentioning that happened during active or reserve duty in the U.S. Marine Corps, the U.S. Navy, the U.S. Coast Guard or allied sister services, usually at sea or across the sea, but not always.

By the way, the sea story "voice" is always low-key conversational no matter what the subject except for matters of well-packaged gender.

Sea stories come in a variety of sizes from a short vignette of only a few paragraphs to a dozen or more typed, single-spaced pages relative to a variety of categories such as those sea stories that typically:

a. Can usually be told comfortably in mixed adult company, including your mom, maiden aunt, and maybe even your Bible-thumping pastor, bless his or her heart.
b. Are told among consenting adults, but probably not your mom, maiden aunt or Bible-thumping pastor because very little if any adult content is usually deleted.
c. Are more appreciated by salty old "sea dog" veterans who were once, or will probably be in the same places or situations someday during his or her tours of duty.

VAH-7, The Point of the Navy Spear, is a combination of Category "a" with a hint of Category "c" just for the heck of it.

2. BACKSTORY

If you have read *"1953: Making A Marine Grunt Warrior"* and/or *"1954: Making A Marine Pilot Warrior"* you are familiar with the contents of this backstory and you may want to skip ahead to Chapter II, The Navy's General LeMay Problems. However, if you would appreciate a timely reminder of the elements that led to this time and place in my Cold War Warrior Trilogy, you may wish to continue reading this backstory.

2.1 1953: MAKING A MARINE GRUNT WARRIOR

I actually enjoyed Boot Camp at the U.S. Marine Corps Recruit Depot, San Diego, California in the spring of 1953. The Marines issued me the best rifle that I had ever fired, a lot of free ammunition, and let me shoot it for weeks at a time at the Camp Mathews rifle range. They also gave me three nutritious meals every day; some of which were fairly decent if you are not too picky and have a lot of condiments handy. But most important of all, they also gave me the opportunity to earn one of the most respected military uniforms on God's green earth. Who would not be proud to wear that uniform?

With all of the calisthenics, marching and other physical and mental exercises all day every day with Recruit Platoon 118 (figure 1), otherwise known as the Wichita (Kansas) Platoon, I was probably in the best physical shape of my life. That included the prior football season when I was playing first string offensive/defensive end, kicking extra points and field goals, and punting for the Kansas junior college champion El Dorado Grizzlies; pulling pipe in the Oil Patch during that sweltering Kansas summer and post-football weekends, as well as playing semi-professional baseball. (figure 2)

A second semester sophomore when I enlisted, I put a full football scholarship at Kansas State University for my junior and senior years on hold, as well as a professional baseball contract with the Boston Red Sox. Somehow I actually believed that I could easily get all of that good stuff back again after a three-year tour of duty in the Marines during the Korean War. Silly me.

Figure 1. Recruit Platoon 118, Day 3 in Boot Camp

Then some optimist in the chain of command thought that I could become a decent Grunt infantry officer, so they sent me to Drill Instructors'

School as the first step in transitioning from enlisted to officer status while most of my platoon went to Korea to get even with the North Korean and Chinese communist hoards. Until that time, an applicant for DI School had to be at least a corporal (I was only a brand new Pfc.), have an officer's IQ (120 points or more), and preferably have combat experience. One out of three did not seem like a promising average to start down that road.

Figure 2. The Author Played Semi-Pro Baseball to Earn Contracts from the Boston Red Sox

At that time, DI School was one of the most difficult and demanding schools in the Marine Corps. On average, about 50 percent of the qualified Marine warriors who were accepted by DI School either flunked out due to the constant written tests and pop quizzes every day, or the constant physical exercising and drilling on the parade grounds. Except for the IQ requirement, I was definitely over my head and I knew it. So I did not go on liberty breaks off the base, memorized the large and very precise *Landing*

Party Manual about all things Marine, and survived the many challenges to become one of only three graduates in my class (figure 3) who were immediately assigned to a recruit platoon although the ranking Gunnery Sergeant (five stripes: three up and two down) hated my guts because he thought I was having too much fun in his extremely serious school.

Actually, when physically overexerted, I sounded like I was laughing every time I sucked-in air during extensive exercises when other guys were tossing their cookies and dropping out of the program. I figured what the heck, you can't please everybody all thetime.

Figure 3. Drill Instructors' School Graduation

As the junior DI with Platoon 205, I worked long hours and darned hard to teach our 75 recruits how to: obey orders; do the "five S's" between reveille and the morning calisthenics before breakfast; march and run together in precise formations; master the basics of being a Marine; spit shine their shoes until they gleamed; iron military creases into their Class "A" shirts (i.e., blouses) and trousers; hike 20 miles into the southern California mountains with full battle gear and only one canteen of water each; shoot M1 rifles accurately at 200, 300, and

500 yard ranges (figure 4); skewer bad guys on the pointy ends of our bayonets if they are dumb enough to get that close (figure 5); throw hand grenades, etc.; and write a letter home to Mom and Pop at least once every Sunday afternoon.

Figure 4. Recruits Firing at the 500-Yard Line at Camp Mathews

Figure 5. Marine Trained Rat

At that time, iconic Marine Colonel, later Major General, Lewis "Chesty" Puller declared that too many of his close air support pilots had not been as aggressive as he wanted during the "Frozen Chosin Reservoir" Campaign in the snow-covered mountains of far northern Korea. Chesty wanted some hard-charging enlisted Marine grunts to become pilots and show some of those ex-Ivy League fraternity boy pilots how close air support should be flown. As a result, 12 enlisted Marines were chosen out of the 194,000 enlisted Marines in the Corps at that time. For some unfathomable darned reason, I was one of that dozen. Say what!

In late September, I was transferred to Naval Air Station Moffett Field near San Jose, California to play football and basketball for the Red Raiders, work as a Military Policeman (MP) on patrol, and a Marine Guard at the super-secret Ames Laboratory where I was cleared to a Secret security clearance although somehow I did not know about that while waiting for my orders to transfer to Pensacola, Florida for pilot training.

The NAS Moffett Field Red Raiders played the Armed Forces Day Football Classic for 1953 on national TV. We lost because our best and only top notch running back broke his leg during war-game maneuvers a couple of days before the game. However, I lucked out because the TV announcer liked my long, accurate punting a lot and said so repeatedly. Over the next few months, I received 11 full football scholarships in the mail from Kansas, Kansas State, Nebraska, Denver, Colorado, Oklahoma State (then Oklahoma A&M) and five other universities that were either on the wrong side of the Rocky Mountains or the Mississippi River. Of course, I chose the wrong school for the wrong reason, but that's another story for another time.

The best part about Moffett Field was finally receiving my Advanced Combat Training with elements of the famous 5th Marine Brigade of the 1st Marine Division that mauled the three Chinese Divisions that were assigned to destroy the 1st Marine Division during the "Frozen Chosin Reservoir" Campaign in North Korea during the terribly harsh winter of 1950/51. Ooooo-raaah! I loved every minute of my combat training in the mountains of northern California. I could not have had better teachers or better examples than the veterans of the 5th Marine Brigade.

2.2. 1954: MAKING A MARINE PILOT WARRIOR

This segment describes NavCad (Naval Cadet) ground school and flight training with vintage, dangerously worn-out, pre-World War II trainer aircraft, the SNJ Texan (figure 6) that accounted for so many accidents including an average of at least one fatality for each month of flight operations at Pensacola in 1954 and early 1955.

Figure 6. Navy SNJ Texan Fighter Training Aircraft

Highlights include my year as the Cadet Battalion Commander; glorious weekends on the famous white sands of Pensacola beach; finally "shooting down" my flight instructor after losing too many mock dogfights with him; being the first NavCad to fly the new T-34 Mentor aircraft (figure 7) while at home on Christmas leave; clobbering the loud-mouthed, irritating boxing instructor in the first round of a three-round demonstration bout; searching the local

Figure 7. USAF T-34 Mentor Trainer Aircraft

night clubs for "my one true love; and being honored as the only NavCad inducted into the Confederate Air Corps (figure 8), which at that time was comprised of only southern-born Marine and Navy gentlemen fighter pilots who fought in World War II and the Korean War. At several of the monthly midnight BBQ and keg parties, it seemed that I was the only pilot there who had not shot down at least one Japanese aircraft during World War II.

My NavCad career-ending crash in a Florida swamp is described from takeoff to heroic rescue by Navy crash crews and Navy Corpsmen who pulled my battered and unconscious body out of the burning, upside-down, submerged wreckage and kept me going until I could breath again.

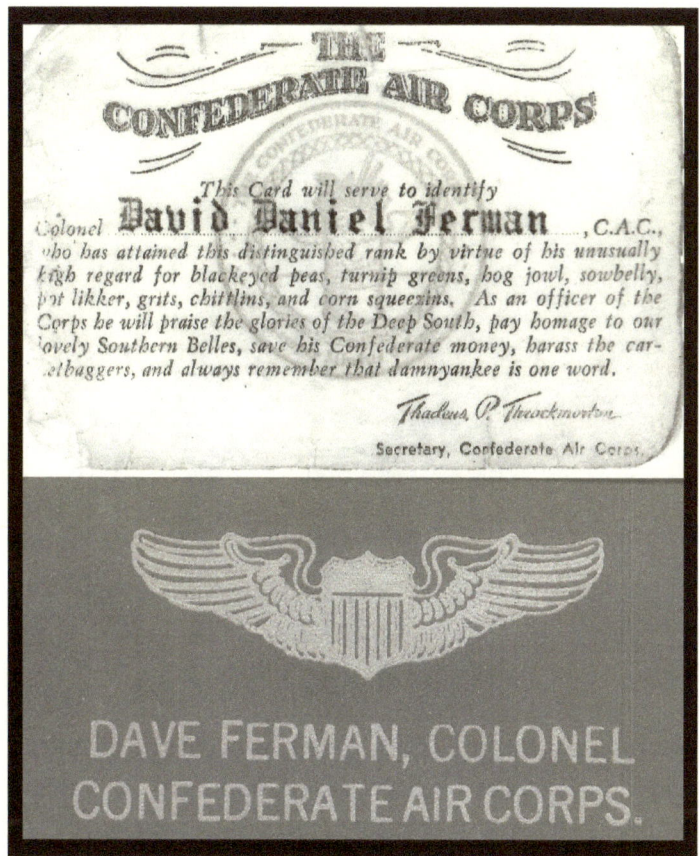

Figure 8. Confederate Air Corps Induction

2.3. THE DAY I CRASHED, BURNED, AND NEARLY DROWNED.

On the day that my SNJ Texan aircraft (figure 9) crashed, burned, and I darn near drowned in the brackish waters of that stale Florida swampy wetland, everything was initially A-Ok. That was, indeed, another fine day for an hour or two of solo aerobatics hijinks in the severe-clear morning sunshine. In my seldom humble opinion, aerial aerobatics in the wild, blue yonder are the most fun that a young cadet pilot can have with his clothes on.

Figure 9. Author With SNJ

Unfortunately, when I added power to begin my takeoff roll, that previously damaged old bird hiccupped, sputtered, and then just sat there on the duty runway blocking traffic. My assigned SNJ did not have enough power to even begin the takeoff roll. So I eased off the manifold pressure and signaled the cadet pilot on the other side of the runway to go ahead and take off before me so that I could checkout that possibly significant hiccup. However, that blockhead just sat there looking at me like a village idiot while the line of SNJs following each of us got longer and longer.

Anxious to get the heck out of the way of the rapidly forming queue, for some darned reason I thought "Aw heck, let's go for broke," and pushed the manifold pressure to full take-off power again. Well darned if I didn't start rolling just as the other cadet woke up and decided to finally do the same thing, so that both of us were accelerating down the runway side by side, but with a fairly safe lateral space between us. That was not as unusual as you might think because I had done that forbidden ploy intentionally on several night takeoffs in order to stick close to Bob, my usual wingman who had a lot better night vision than yours truly. So I figured that mildly iffy situation was no big deal; that is, it wasn't until my main landing gear wheels lifted off the runway and my SNJ lost the lateral friction between my rubber tires and the runway tarmac.

Immediately, my right wing snapped up from the horizontal and came very close to being fully vertical. Startled as the dickens, I was sure that I was just about to drag my left wing-tip on the tarmac, cartwheel right there on the runway, and bow out in a big ugly ball of explosive fire and black greasy smoke. At the same time, I felt like a huge, open hand was underneath my airplane pushing me hard to the left toward the swamp and that other cadet's SNJ as well.

Instinctively, I slammed full right joy stick and kicked hard right rudder, but my plane continued flying to the left while I crossed directly over the other cadet with my left wingtip passing within inches of his open canopy. As I looked straight down at him from only a few inches more than the length of my SNJ's left wing above him, he seemed to go catatonic as he stared straight up at me as if I was the avenging angel of death. That poor guy had really big blue eyes. I could see them as plain as day.

Unable to recover, I grabbed my radio microphone and yelled "Mayday, Mayday, MAYDAY, I'm going down. I'M GOING DOWN!" The control tower operator calmly responded: "Ahh Roger. Where are you, Mayday?" I yelled back at him: "I'm right in front of you, DAMMIT!" Again, the tower calmly replied: "Ah yes, I can see you now."

Days later, at the post-accident analysis meeting, I recognized the tower operator—Roe Messner, who later married Tammy Faye Baker the televangelist—because he was our batboy when his older brother Bobby and I played for the championship T-Men Little League baseball team in Wichita, Kansas, way back in the summer of 1945.

Like somebody important often said: "It is, indeed, a very small world."

With my SNJ still out of control and barely flying in that extremely dangerous attitude—especially since I was flying that close to the ground—I was sure that I would "buy the farm for Mom and Dad," and was just about to be null and void. With the manifold pressure still firewalled at full takeoff power, I had already passed over the edge of the swamp that laid parallel to the far north end of the runway.

After pulling up my landing gear and the rest of my wing flaps, my wings rotated through straight and level, then further to the right for a change as I stayed fairly low to pick-up as much airspeed as possible. Just when I was sure that I was about to snap into a steep-turn stall and flip over inverted to crash into the brackish black water only a matter of feet below me, my sick old SNJ somehow righted itself once again. At that faster airspeed, my wounded old bird headed for altitude like a homesick angel.

As terror turned into relief, I knew that I was still in deep doo doo, but at least I had beaten the odds one more time. However, I wasn't out of the frying pan yet.

The Flight Safety Officer—a Navy lieutenant commander who was a friend as well as one of the good ol' boys in our still somewhat clandestine Confederate Air Corps back when the CAC only accepted Navy and Marine fighter pilots—he got on the horn and told me to take that sick old junker to altitude and give it a stall test. So I carefully flew up to about 9,000 feet altitude and then stalled my SNJ in the normal wings-level attitude.

Bad news: the darned thing stalled with a violent snap to the left. That was not anywhere near normal. At more than 22 knots of air speed too soon, that was a complete surprise. Then, it did not recover from that spin within a turn and a half as advertised. In fact, it spun continuously, totally out of control until I was several thousand feet below the 5,000-foot mandatory bailout altitude before I could get it sorted out and somewhat under control by picked up air speed by dumping my SNJ's nose even further downward.

Apparently perplexed, or maybe he was just stalling to buy some more time to launch the Air/Sea Rescue's PBY amphibious aircraft, the Safety Officer told me to fly back up to a 12,000-foot altitude and stall that sick old junker again. However, that time he wanted me to read him the decreasing airspeed numbers down to the exact onset of that unusually violent, snapping stall beginning with the wings level.

It was gut-check time. I had to maintain a faster air speed while gaining altitude or my SNJ could have snapped into a stall on the way back up to altitude. A chilling revelation, I realized what could have happened the first time when I had not understood the aerodynamic danger of the normal climbing speed in that condition. But like any good Marine, I followed orders and did what I was told to do, and had darn near essentially the same results.

The consensus quick-look analysis indicated that SNJ was no longer capable of flying at about 22 knots above the normal stalling speed in a wings-level and otherwise clean configuration. Furthermore, it was not a good idea to execute a Navy/Marine full-stall carrier-type landing, or even approach the duty runway in the standard racetrack landing pattern where it could stall even sooner in a turn; i.e., possibly at 30 knots or more above the normal stalling speed and too darned low to recover from that stall and subsequent spin.

Also, I was fairly sure that I would have to bail out after falling more than eight spinning turns or so. However, I really did not want to do that, especially since one of my guys had recently bailed out at below 5,000 feet and was killed when his parachute did not fully open. That was definitely on my mind at that time, so I stuck with that sick old SNJ a lot longer than I should have. Silly me.

The next thing that I knew, the Safety Officer told me for the record what we both already knew: that out-of-rig, old, pre-WW II hunk of worn-out junk had undoubtedly been grossly boogered on the previous flight, and was not only unsafe to fly, but it was really unsafe to land. He advised me that I should trim it for straight and level flight at cruising speed, aim it south over the gulf coast and bail out. By that time, a WW-II PBY amphibious Air/Sea Rescue plane was already in the air and waiting for me to splash.

However, since my flight was originally not meant to be an over-water flight, my Mae West flotation vest was still hanging in my equipment locker back at the hangar. So if you think the Safety Officer's plan was a comforting thought, you have another thought coming to you.

That was particularly bad news because at times of severe stress—like that flight most definitely was—I would apparently pump way too much adrenaline in my body, and my perception of time would go from real-time to slow-motion time like I described in far more detail in one of my earlier books: *Ghosts That I Have Known*. Therefore, if I jumped and the parachute once again became a streamer instead of fully deploying, that fall to eternity would possibly seem to go on and on for a heck of a long time before I would suddenly meet my Maker. However, if I jumped over water, splashed in the bay and then got tangled in my parachute riser lines without my Mae West flotation vest, I would be damned if I did jump and damned if I didn't jump. Either way, my $10,000 military life insurance would probably "buy the farm" for Mom and Dad.

The Safety Officer and I talked a while about various crash list fundamentals, but I was still not enthusiastic about bailing out. Finally, I told him quite brashly—but as one Confederate Air Corps (CAC) Colonel to another CAC Colonel rather than as a noncommissioned NavCad to a Navy Lt. Commander—that I was in command of that aircraft, and I choose to attempt to land it while flying straight and level at a much faster airspeed than normal. I really did not give a flip how my friend the Safety Officer would explain that whole rain dance to the Admiral's Safety Board, but I wanted to be there when it happened.

After about 30 minutes of messing around to get our arms wrapped around all of the potential contingencies and survival procedures, the Safety Officer cleared every other aircraft out of the north/south landing pattern, and allowed a straight-in approach from about 15 miles north of the runway so that my wings could stay as level as possible while my airspeed would be slowly reduced.

NOTE: the off-shore breeze had shifted almost 180 degrees to an on-shore breeze while we were gabbing about my mortality. I would be attempting to land toward the swamp rather than away from those swampy wet lands. Welcome to Florida.

Fortunately, an instructor pilot in an identical SNJ joined up and flew a loose formation on my right wing and helped to talk me down to a landing by constantly telling me my exact air speed so that I would not lose track, suddenly stall, and fall out of the air at an altitude too low to recover. That way, I was able to keep my head up and on a swivel while descending without running up too much or too little air speed in the process.

That's a pretty good trick for a NavCad student pilot who, aside from little more than an hour flying the new Beechcraft T-34 Mentor aircraft that only the Air Force had at that time, and about the same pittance in a much hotter T-28 Trojan aircraft with my CAC brothers. However, both of those aircraft were equipped with tricycle landing gear while I had only landed SNJ tail-dragging aircraft with a comfortably slow, full-stall landing and not by greasing the aircraft onto the runway Air Force style like I was attempting to do with a very sick aircraft.

So I opened my canopy, lowered my seat as far down as it would go, pulled my shoulder and lap harnesses even tighter, said yet another fervent Act of Contrition, asked Holy Joe, my Guardian Angel to get to work on my case muy pronto, and I may have offered up my first-born child in the bargain as well.

Then I turned very carefully onto my straight-in approach beginning about 15 miles north of the duty runway. Fresh out of options and thoroughly committed to try to land that gut-shot old junker one more time, I muttered "Houkah hei" into my microphone, which is shorthand for a Plains Indian adage loosely translated as "this is as good a day to die as any." From our monthly, late-night CAC steak and keg parties, my CAC brother, the Safety Officer, received my message loud and clear. I figured that I had no choice but to go for broke.

Flying at a bit more than 28 knots faster than specifications on my final approach, I knew that I would be darned lucky to touch down in the first third of that very short 6,000-foot north-to-south runway.

However, when I tried but could not touch down in the first third at that excessive airspeed, and barely within the second third of that very short runway, I knew that I was in a world of hurt, and that abnormal landing attempt probably would not end well for me.

As my pal Bill Brill's mama often said: "Pain hurts."

Actually, I initially touched down somewhere between the second and the final third of the duty runway, but by that time I was too darned close to my new 100-knot stalling speed—the normal stalling speed was about 78 knots—so taking a wave-off to go around and try again was probably not a survivable option at that altitude. So I cut my power completely, slammed down on the runway way too hard and too fast, ballooned a couple of times, and passed between two Navy fire trucks that were racing down each side of the runway with their pedals to the metal. At a little more than 100 knots—about 114 miles per hour—I passed between them like they were standing still. Heck, I nearly blew their doors off.

A few seconds later, I bounced over the south end of the runway while still moving at about 100 miles per hour. At that speed, when hurtling through a brackish swamp that was once a densely forested wetland, a junior birdman's future can be measured in seconds. Having no control except for a faint semblance of brakes since I was bouncing into the air so much, I slammed into a large, sturdy swamp tree that violently snapped me to the right and took off my right wing at the fuselage with a head-banging, neck-popping impact that pretty much boogered every muscle and tendon in my body.

Still standing on the brakes with the joystick anchored back in my lap with both hands, I vaguely remember hitting a second tree at about midpoint on my left wing, which suddenly, violently snapped me in the other direction and tore off that wing as well as the engine cowling and other susceptible parts. That spun me around like a whirling dervish on steroids—maybe a full 360 degrees a couple of times; I really don't know because it happened so fast—which removed my propeller and engine at the lord mounts directly in front of my cockpit cage, and then smashed my entire tail assembly into a whole gaggle of fluttering fragments and metal strips.

Immediately after that, the momentum threw what was left of the cockpit cage with me in it against a huge tree trunk head-on and dropped my SNJ's gaping-open front end down against that tree in at least waist-high, brackish, swamp water. That flipped what was left of the torn-up fuselage cage straight forward into an upside-down stack of scrambled parts.

Having been snapped around violently again and again despite my tightened shoulder and lap harnesses, I lost track of the time line, but I would guess that the entire destruction of that weary old junker probably took only a few seconds from the point of hitting the first tree and then spinning violently and much too fast in both directions until the sudden, head-snapping stop when I hit the last tree to crush my open canopy and smash against that tree's massive trunk where I mercifully lost all consciousness while hanging upside down with my head and shoulders fully submerged under that black, brackish swamp water.

Thank God for the sturdy crash bar just behind my head, and for that magnificent Navy crash crew in their silver moon suits who got to the scene of the accident almost as soon as I did. All things considered, that was quite a slick trick for them to somehow follow the path that I had cut through that still densely wooded, mud-sucking swamp so quickly, but thank God that they somehow did that trick in what must have been record time.

I do wish that someone had taken a movie to show the world just how great those Navy crash crew guys did their very difficult job. But take it from the guy who darned near drowned without even knowing it, I am darned sure that I would not have survived without their fast, efficient, life-saving heroics.

I have vague memories of drifting in and out of consciousness in a world where every part of my body hurt like the dickens while I snorted and puked vile liquids in and out of my nose and mouth as a surge of deep sorrow enveloped me. That was not how I thought heaven would be.

Quickly and efficiently, those crash crew guys in their otherworldly silver suits either released or cut my harness straps to drop me head-first onto something hard and substantial like a stump further below the surface of that nauseating, crappy tasting swamp water. Then, some more Navy guys in firefighting gear appeared out of nowhere and toted me on a stretcher through the swamp to the meat wagon as little patches of gasoline ignited around us on the surface of the rancid, dark water. I vaguely remember them as bright flickers on the blackish surface of the shiny swamp water that seemed like hundreds of flickering candles swirling around me. However, the accident report said the fire was a bit more intense than that.

I was so darned glad to be finally on the ground—even mucky, swampy ground—that the encircling thousand "candles" did not bother me at all. To me, they were pretty lights that were somehow really comforting like great big clusters of candles at Midnight Mass on Christmas Eve rather than the solemn serenity of a Requiem Funeral Mass.

With everything finally under Navy control, I drifted off to La La Land again.

Go Navy. I love you guys.

Like Mr. Cowboy, the battered old night clerk at the Royal Hotel in El Dorado, Kansas, often described a hard day of breaking broncos or branding cattle back in his prime: "I felt like I had been rode hard and put away wet." I could not have said it better.

2.4. YOU SCRATCH MY BACK AND I'LL SCRATCH YOURS

I awoke in the main Navy hospital at the Pensacola Flight Training Command. As I was recovering from another major concussion as well as many other generally debilitating aches and pains all over my body ("pain hurts!"), the doctors found indisputable evidence of past bruises and abrasions to my noggin in days of yore. Immediately if not sooner, my ticket for further stick time as a Navy/Marine pilot was cancelled.

Heck fire, the evidence of that original damage was apparently there all of the time if anyone had looked during my many physicals, and may still be there today. Then, as they huddled in the hall outside my hospital room, I could hear several of those doctors grumbling about such as: "how in the heck did that guy ever get here in the first place;" as well as harsh incriminations such as "bogus enlistment." I figured that I was in deep kimchi, but was in no condition to get up and run for it.

As I had explained ad nauseum that before I enlisted, I reported my medical history as best I could. However, on the repeated advice of my recruiter, Sgt. Kuhn, who filled out my medical record because my writing hand was broken and in a plaster cast from playing junior college football, I did not add anything that was not asked. I joined the Marines so that I could go to Korea and get even with the North Korean and Chinese S.O.B's who had killed and wounded several of my good friends back home. It was as simple as that.

After that, everything kind of flowed along rapidly and beyond my control. Those three unexpected high IQ tests in one year that led to Mensa and sidetracked me to OCS, but that was okay with me after the Cease Fire in Korea ruined Plan A. I did not have a Plan B.

Everyone involved in my last flight got together a couple of days after I was released from the hospital, but I did not see any accident photos so some of those guys figured that those probably were not processed yet. Yeah, right. Additionally, no one told me which sum'bitch flew and boogered that SNJ just before it was assigned to me. I'm damned sure that they knew, but no one squealed on him so he had to be someone with a pot full of influence. That bastard knowingly tore up the control cables' rigging system and the flaps so darned badly on his last landing, yet he did not report that critical damage. So much for that BS NavCad Honor System for self-reporting damaged aircraft. Whose naïve, stupid, cotton-picking idea was that, anyway?

However, the Safety Officer, my Confederate Air Corps pal, did verify that the cables, etc. of the whole danged control system were fatally out of rig and there was nothing that I could have done about it after I was in the air. In fact, they figured that I was darned lucky just to get that gut-shot old junker into the air in the first place because I probably should have crashed during taking off.

I mentioned that they should tell me something that I did not already know, like who the heck flew that aircraft and clobbered it before my flight, thereby screwing it up so incredibly badly, and then did not file a squawk to get the darned thing overhauled or torn down for spare parts as a shop queen. If I had known that SOB's name, I damned sure would have burned down his barn.

But after all of that was said and done, the thing that really fried my hide the most was why the heck wasn't I diverted from that minimum, inadequate 6,000-foot-long runway at NAS Sauffley Field to the 18,000-foot long runways at Eglin Air Force Base only a few minutes by air to the east of the Pensacola Flight Training Command. I'll bet that I could have flown that beat-up, old hunk of junk directly onto those three-mile long runways—versus our puny little 6,000-foot runways—at a safe airspeed approximating our standard cruising speed.

I'll bet that would have made that 100-knot stalling speed immaterial. If so, I could now be a retired Marine Aviator despite all of my warts, and the U.S. Navy would have had one more gut-shot old junker SNJ to use as a shop queen until the brand new, delightful-to-fly BeechCraft T-34 Mentor aircraft would finally arrive.

Ah well, as they often said in the bowels of the ancient Roman Coliseum: "non illigitimus nehil carborundum." That translates, I believe, to: "Don't let the bastards get you down." Do I hear another "Aaa-men?" I certainly hope so.

After all was said and done, no wonder that I finally decided to play nice with the U.S. Navy so that would soon be sorted out. The ultimate moral of this story: when dealing with officers and gentlemen, is to get it in writing.

But then, again, what could possibly go wrong?

2.5. AN OFFER I COULD NOT REFUSE

When I was still at the NAS Pensacola hospital, a couple of senior Navy officers who showed neither rank nor any identification on their obviously borrowed, ill-fitting, white, hospital coats—but sporting the command presence of top dog authority galore—came to my room, excused the pretty nurse who was giving me a thorough and delightful sponge bath in bed, shut the door, and made me an offer that I could not/better not refuse. Actually, those senior officers did not give me a whole lot of choice.

Essentially their offer boiled down to me scratching their backs and they reciprocating by scratching mine while simultaneously over-looking my hot-to-trot, naïve young-guy, faux pas while trying to get even with the Chinese and North Korean bad guys. If I agreed to these unidentified officers' offer to join a troubled Navy atom bomber squadron to "observe everything that takes place within sight or hearing," and report back to some flag officer identified only as "the Boss".

According to these two steely eyed characters, if I played ball with them, I would eventually be discharged as a Marine Staff Sergeant. That would be a huge perk at that time, which I understand is now standard for all Marine NavCads who have at least 100 hours of flight time when grounded. Additionally, I would do no time in the active reserves, and there would be no more flack about my bad/nasty impulsive bogus enlistment just to kill a few insignificant bad guys in Korea. Also, I would get an all-expenses-paid exotic cruise in the beautiful Mediterranean Sea with all of the free coffee that I could drink 24/7, the GI Bill benefits, the VA medical benefits, and other benefits too mentionable to be numerous, or words to that effect.

I didn't know if it was that Mensa thing; or my special relationship with the Admiral during about a year when I was the Cadet Battalion Commander, or our midnight BBQ and keg parties every month when Admiral and cadet were both equal colonels in the Confederate Air Corps for a few hours, or because I crammed in time in my already hectic schedule to play defensive end and punter on the Admiral's football team; or that I "shot down" my instructor in a mock dog fight using a trick that I learned from Captain Fisher who was once Pappy Boyington's wingman; or because I decked the boxing instructor after he called Joe Bolling and I "girls," or because I'm left handed and had a good tan. Heck, I don't know what it was that lit those senior officers' fire, but they would not take "No Sir" for their offer.

When I woke up the next morning, I called the Commanding Officer of the Marine Detachment at Pensacola on the phone to ask for an appointment with him to discuss my nebulous situation. Unfortunately, he was traveling so his secretary/office pinky transferred my call to the Marine Personnel Office where somebody with a strong vocal command presence but a sympathetic attitude told me that he was sure that I could come back to the Marines right away, but I would need to re-enlist for three more years to do that.

Time was of the essence. I had to make a big decision, and do it right away. So we talked for a while, and as a surprising aside comment the Marine Personnel guy mentioned that since I wanted to get back to college as soon as possible, I would get out in just 10 months if I would take the Navy offer. If I re-enlisted with the Marines, I would not get back to college until the fall semester of 1958 or the spring semester of 1959.

Long story short, after quite a bit of give and take, I eventually took those Navy guys at their honorable word, settled with a hand-shake to get rid of them, and went back to sleep. What the heck, after all was said and done, I did owe my life to a couple of hard-charging Navy crash crews and a whole bunch of Navy corpsmen who just flat would not give up even after I had been under water for something like four minutes.

I pride myself on always paying off my debts.

A word to the wise: when negotiating with "officers and gentlemen" like those guys, get it in writing. A rookie in such matters: I did not do that. I was just so darned happy to still be breathing.

That's my story, and I'm going to stick with it.

II. THE U.S. NAVY'S GENERAL LEMAY PROBLEM

Later, those same nameless senior officers stopped by to explain that the Navy had a big problem, and how I fit into the overall equation. As I learned then and later in bits and pieces, apparently few if any of the Navy atom bomber squadrons were passing their Combat Readiness evaluations. In fact, one Navy atom bomber squadron was kicked off an aircraft carrier for being incompetent and "downright dangerous" according to that ship's captain. Because of that and other factors, the Navy was in danger of losing all of the congressional funds for atom bomb delivery to the U.S. Air Force.

That faux pas could eventually eliminate the need for Navy aircraft carriers. USAF General Curtis LeMay, fresh from ending WW II with just two atom bombs, was knocking on the Navy's door, and could soon kick down that door to take all of the Navy's congressional appropriations for atom bomb delivery.

That could, quite conceivably, be the wave of the future.

1. PLAN "A"

In a flat-out panic, the Navy had sent teams of their best multi-engine pilots to assess the many problems with the atom bomber squadrons so that the Navy Department could divine a timely solution. But the wheels came off that wagon when the investigators and the investigated invariably got together, compared notes, knocked their fraternal Naval Academy rings loud and proud, exchanged sea stories, and "drank quantities untold." Then the investigators penned glowing reports to their superiors, military and civilian, while every one of the Navy atom bomber squadrons continued to fail their Combat Readiness evaluations by disturbing margins. So much for Navy Plan "A."

2. PLAN "B"

Confused by the conflicts between the Plan "A" analyses and the reality of the atom bomber squadrons' actual lack of combat readiness, and even more in danger of losing their beloved congressional appropriations than before, the Navy Department formed Plan "B;" an elite Navy "Blue Ribbon" Team comprised of senior command pilots, time-and-motion geeks, bean counters, logisticians, and I don't know who all. These leaders of that team apparently went through essentially the same rain dances as the first group of highly qualified although apparently biased investigators. Under their microscopes, apparently darned near everything looked pretty darn spiffy to them as well.

So why didn't the Combat Readiness evaluations of the atom bomber squadrons reflect those opinions from on high? Nobody had the answers, but every flag officer at the top of the Navy food chain was in a state of profound panic. This conundrum was serious business in the office of the Secretary of the Navy. In fact, at that time, General LeMay's Air Force was scheming for an all-services arrangement in which they would be in charge of all aviation assets and aviation personnel in all services, and would receive all congressional aviation funds for personnel and aviation assets currently under the command of the Army, Navy, Marines, Coast Guard, National Guard and Reserves. You name it, if it flew or had anything to do with flying, the Air Force wanted it.

3. PLAN "C"

Finally, in utter desperation, Naval Intelligence sent out less obvious, undeclared observers who were not fraternal brothers in the wild blue yonder. These guys were covertly placed in positions to observe squadron operations and report their findings back to the senior command/flag/decision-making echelons. Plan "C" was me, and undoubtedly other guys like me in the other atom bomber squadrons. Overtly low-level guys (I was rated an airman, the equivalent of a Marine corporal) whom nobody would ever suspect. However, I did not know if others like me were actually out there or not. That tidbit was way above my pay grade or my mission description.

Anyway, I got the rose for atom bomber squadron VAH-7, and supposedly no one in that squadron or onboard the various aircraft carriers was privy to that game plan or my particular mission. I don't know about the Admirals on both aircraft carriers that I would serve on, but I would eventually have personal contact with both (each eventually did me a significant favor) although my primary mission was never discussed with either one of them.

That began a whole new line of work which would keep me up to my giblets in authorized skullduggery and legerdemain until I was discharged a few weeks early for spring football practice at Denver University in the spring of 1956. But what the heck, that plan kind of, sort of, almost matched my original schedule when I enlisted in the Marines.

Anyway, back at the Pensacola hospital, after yet another pep talk from those two steely eyed but still unidentified senior Navy officers, I was actually eager to jump off the darned porch and run with the big dogs.

So once again, highly and appropriately trained enlisted men did another of the jobs that the officers either could not, or would not do.

Good luck finding that in the U.S. Navy historic records.

III. METAMORPHOSIS OF A COVERT APPRENTICE

1. NAS PATUXENT RIVER WAS SOFTBALL HEAVEN.

When I arrived at NAS Patuxent River, Maryland, I reported to the base softball (fast pitch) coach at the light-duty dormitory and spa. An older "mustang" lieutenant (i.e., he came up through the enlisted ranks) was expecting me and, curiously, right away he asked me why I did not sign-up with the Boston Red Sox farm system after they offered me contracts when I was playing semi-pro baseball in both 1951 and 1952. I was pretty darned surprised that he knew anything about that as well as so much more about my athletic pedigree. So I explained that according to the NCAA rules of that time, if I took one thin dime for playing any sport professionally, I would be ineligible to play amateur sports to pay for my room, board, books and tuition on a college baseball or football scholarship.

That was the reason why the Roscam Realtors semi-pro baseball team in Wichita, Kansas paid me in six packs of cold beer for playing baseball while every other guy on that team was paid with green folding money although I had one of the better batting averages on the team. For some vague, inscrutable reason, that arrangement was apparently okay with the NCAA Powers That Be, and certainly made the after-game parties a lot more entertaining.

My explanation seemed to satisfy the coach's curiosity because he never brought it up again. Even before I could unpack my sea bag, he took me to the base field house, and gave me new practice and game uniforms, cleats, sox, jocks, hat and a beautiful, royal blue, top-of-the-line warmup jacket. Then we went to the practice field for a workout at first base with the Pax River softball team, and an extra-long session in the batting cage. Best of all, in those days the athletes' mess at Pax River had the same menu as the officers' mess. That was a heck of an improvement.

I've got to admit that I surprised myself by hitting pretty well after about 10 minutes of re-orientation to underhanded pitching. Considering that I had not played men's fast-pitch softball since I was working the night shift at BeechCraft in Wichita, somehow it all came back to me pretty darned fast. I tightened my stance and my swing, and shifted my weight forward to hit line drives rather than taking a longer step toward the pitcher with my right foot like I would if going for the fence in baseball. Fairly soon, I was getting pretty darned comfortable at the plate and hitting the ball where I wanted it to go almost like an extended field game of fast-pitch pepper ball.

Fielding was no problem either. My new Rawlings T-70-RY trapper first-baseman's mitt, which was identical to the one that I took from my friend Dwayne Wilson of the Boston Red Sox (he had owed me $100 for several years while I was in the military; I don't remember why), but was then stolen off the playing field at Pensacola Mainside during a game that was played, officiated and watched exclusively by current and future "officers and gentlemen." What does that tell you? Yeah. Me too.

That new mitt was perfect for softball right out of the box. It needed very little breaking in but lots of neat's-foot oil. My new team mates were darned decent fielders and several of the infielders had pretty good throwing arms. That top-of-the-line first-baseman mitt helped me look much better than I expected, whether stretching for a high throw or blocking the ball down in the dirt. I still had my cannon left arm to throw out runners clear across the field at third base. However, I was still hurting a bit and slightly hobbled from that crash in the swamp weeks earlier, so I wasn't quite as quick running the bases.

However, that was no big deal because I never was a base-stealing threat. Fortunately, that concussion had receded so that my gourd was no longer feeling like it was full of water. Hell's bells, I figured that I was darn near physically ready to play softball. No one was more surprised than me.

The very next day, I was the starting first baseman for Navy Pax River in the military softball league and remained unchallenged for that position. No wonder the coach had hustled my tryout on my very first day onboard. These guys took softball seriously. Pretty soon, I did too although at first I was exhausted after each game.

We played Army, Air Force, Marine and other Navy teams two or three times a week plus the weekend tournaments. They were all very good fast-pitch softball teams that would be rated at least "Double A" if softball would ever become a professional sport like baseball. These guys played good fast-pitch softball, and we were having a grand ol' time. That's a heck of a good game when played as it should be.

No doubt about it, Pax River was softball Hog Heaven. Unlike playing football in the Marines or at Pensacola when I had other full-time duties and college-level football was extracurricular, I had no other duties or responsibilities worth mentioning at Pax River. Essentially, all I did was play softball, rest whenever I could, and smile a lot.

Right out of the box, we were winning ball games against teams that I heard had recently ruled the roost. We always had large, vocal, fun-loving crowds of Navy and Marine guys and gals as well as their families cheering us at each home game and a few of the road games as well. With the backstop so close behind home plate for softball, at every home game growing gaggles of Navy Waves and Marine BAM softball groupies were offering darn near everything but their first born kids if we would keep hitting and winning.

Then, one foggy morning, I received orders to report to the Air Intelligence Officer at Squadron VAH-7, which was located at the far end of the base. No way! I was really very happy where I was. Hells bells, I was giddy about my current duties. I had finally found my proverbial nest on the ground.

So I pulled the coach's chain, and he went to bat for me with his commanding officer who, with his whole family, were softball fans and never missed a home game. That officer shook out his chain of command, but was just flat over-ruled anyway. So I talked to the Master Chief of the NAS Pax River Personnel Office, who was also a big softball fan and attended almost every home game with his wife and little kids. However, that too was no sale because in the Chief's exact words: "I don't know why, Dave, but it's already a done deal. There is nothing I can do about it. Lord knows I gave it my best shot."

Right away, I knew who was pulling these particular strings and why, but I was having so much fun that I naively hoped for a reprieve with the shadowy Powers That Be, or maybe even a do-over. So I hopped on the base bus over to the VAH-7 squadron campus and pleaded my case with their Chief Petty Officer in Personnel. A good guy who also looked familiar from past softball games, he explained that the squadron was a special unit (I already knew it was an atom bomber squadron) that was going to be operating in the Mediterranean very soon.

It just so happened that an essential and highly critical slot had just opened in the Air Intelligence Office that had to be filled immediately if not sooner and, surprise, surprise, I filled that bill to a "T." Hell's bells, when I read it, that job description almost looked like it was written just for me. In fact, the text was so specific that I wondered if it had my serial number somewhere in the fine print of that description. It wasn't, of course, but darned near everything else was.

As the Chief reminded me: I had held a Secret security clearance at the Ames Laboratory on the NAS Moffett Field campus so, all things considered, that clearance had already been reinstated, Top Secret was just around the corner, and I could hit the ground running. That was a big deal back then because that security clearance usually took weeks and even months to be approved to that level.

My aviation background could be applied in several ways within the squadron, and my military GED (civilian IQ) indicated that I could probably handle the massive bow wave of information that had to be absorbed and then utilized precisely within a very short lead time. Probably the most important factor of all, I was immediately available to fill that critical empty slot before the squadron deployed overseas.

That afternoon, my Rawlings first baseman's mitt was packed away in the bottom of my sea bag when I reported to the VAH-7 Air Intelligence Officer. Recess was over. A crash course was in session. No pun intended.

2. AIR INTELLIGENCE ALA FIRE HOSE

All day and most evenings, I worked my fanny off to learn everything I could about the current Mark-7 and the upcoming Mark-15 atom bombs, as well as the Navy's sole, viable delivery system, the too-soon obsolete and much flawed AJ-2 Savage atom bomber (figure 10) which was then disguised as an aerial refueling tanker to fool the Soviets and everybody else.

Figure 10. AJ-2 Savage Bomber

That daunting task included everything from mission planning and tactical/strategic coordination; background and current tactical situations; the various procedural protocols from handling each of those two atom bombs to operating unique encryption communications equipment; setup, making, reading, and maintaining various aerial radar maps; preflight and post-flight briefings and debriefing protocols by the numbers; analyses six ways from Sunday; applicable specifications and checklists; and a metric pot full of related data crammed in between. Learning all of that in a matter of weeks was like drinking water out of a fire hose turned on full blast. Except for the aviation component, I was swamped up to my eyeballs in new concepts, regulations, equipment and Top Secret stuff galore.

3. BIG BAD BOMB CHECKOFF LIST

Several weeks before VAH-7 deployed overseas, one morning the Squadron Executive Officer (X.O.) asked me to type the 16-page Top-Secret check-off list for arming, disarming and handling the new Mark 15 atom bomb because both office pinkies (i.e., clerks) were on pre-deployment leave. Naturally, I told him with as straight a face as I could muster, that I could not type worth a flip. However, he had already done his due diligence, checked my personnel file, and knew that I could type pretty darned good since high school. What the heck, he was between a rock and a hard place, so he was reaching for any straw that he could find. That straw was me.

So the Squadron Intelligence Officer, my boss, gave me the handwritten notes and check lists, reams of meticulously counted paper and blue stencils, a stencil printing machine with the big roller and a hand crank (the latest and greatest reproduction technology at that time), a loaded Colt M1911 model .45-caliber pistol and a box of ammo in case of an extended shoot-'em-up on campus overnight (really?). Then they locked me in our Air Intelligence suite with an armed Marine guard posted outside the door.

Lunch, supper and breakfast from the chow hall were delivered on trays along with a gaggle of extra snacks to pacify me until I finally finished typing and copying those lists perfectly. No mistakes or strikeovers were allowed, but that produced more mistakes and strikeovers than usual. One strike-over or any other glitch ruined any page, and I would have to suck it up and start over again on that page.

About half way through the next morning, my boss, the Squadron Intelligence Officer (I will call him Ed for reasons that will become apparent much later) and I accounted for every single sheet of paper, stencil, handwritten note and even blank sheets of paper. Then I signed the paper trail of Top Secret documents over to Ed, returned the .45-caliber pistol, and even counted the number of bullets in the ammo box.

A little later, I was walking down the hall when our Commanding Officer (C.O.) stopped me to get acquainted and asked if I was going to go on leave before our deployment. If so, the last bus to Washington, D.C. was leaving in about three hours. Heck fire, I never guessed that I could take a leave to go home in the middle of my Air Intelligence training, but this guy was our C.O. and if he said taking a leave to go home was okay, I figured that it probably was okay. So I took a shot. I was hungry for Mom's home cooking and wanted to pet my dog. I had not rubbed Taffy's tummy since the past Christmas.

In a Navy atomic bomber squadron, about a dozen offices had to signoff before I could go home on leave. However, before overseas deployments, sudden leaves are common, so about 90 minutes later, I had all but the Squadron Intelligence Officer's signature. Since he was my boss, that should have been a piece of cake. But when I went back to our office, a sign on the door read "Do Not Disturb."

In a hurry, I knocked on the locked door anyway and yelled so Ed would know that it was me. However, he yelled back through the door that he could not let me in that room until he finished an important task. "Come back in an hour" he yelled. I did not have an extra hour, so with the clock ticking and my urge to see my family expanding exponentially, I kicked the door open and found him hand collating the pages that I had just typed and printed.

I was laughing so hard that I had to hang onto a big wall-mounted fire extinguisher in the hallway to keep from falling to the floor. Sheepishly, ol' Ed told me that he knew that the procedure was frivolous, but that was the letter of the law and he was stuck with it. When I finally stopped laughing, I told him that it was okay because I had not looked at the Top Secret check-off list while I was typing and reproducing the pages.

By the way, one copy had my name on it so if I had not been going on leave, I would have gotten my own copy the next day anyway. I also figured that my hole card trumped his silly procedure because: (1), I had the signed permission of our C.O., (2) my sea bag was packed, and (3) I had a bus to catch. Game, set, match.

I caught that darned bus just as the driver was closing the doors to leave the base.

4. BE IT EVER SO HUMBLE…

When I arrived home, Mom asked me what I had been doing in VAH-7, and what was I going to be doing with "those airplanes" (i.e., the AJ-2 Savage bombers). Of course, I could not tell her what I was doing because that was classified Top Secret at that time. I had to keep everything under my hat. But wouldn't you know, that set off her "curious mama" mode, and she would not let up as long as I was at home. We could be eating a great home-cooked meal, and when I asked Mom to pass the butter, she invariably said something like: "I will if you tell me what you are doing with those airplanes" or words to that effect. All day, every day and into the night, she would ask me the same questions.

Dad tried to help me out by telling Mom that she should give me a break and quit asking questions that I obviously could not answer. But then, Mom would retort: "If you can't tell your mother, who can you tell?" Of course, the answer was "no-damn-body," but of course I did not say that to Mom.

As she had done so often when we were kids, Mom climbed those steep, narrow stairs to my room on our second floor on her crutches to search through everything in my room. She would not be denied. If she would have learned anything about VAH-7 and our atom bombers as the point of the U.S. spear in the Mediterranean Theater, that would probably be all over the neighborhood and very likely in the next edition of the Wichita Beacon newspaper the next day.

You see, the Navy declared that the fact that VAH-7 was an atom bomber squadron and not an air-to-air refueling tanker squadron was classified Top Secret. My being an Air Intelligence guy in VAH-7 was classified as a Secret. At Pax River, everyone in our squadron wore a special photo ID badge with a color-coded bar to clearly designate whatever each individual's level of clearance. All of us who worked directly with the atom bombs and the flight crews had a bright yellow horizontal stripe on our badges that designated Top Secret at a glance. In addition, several strands of 14-carot gold thread were sewn into every Top Secret badge before they were laminated within a sealed plastic cover. However, gold was worth only about twenty dollars an ounce back then.

Right after I got home, I found my Top Secret badge inside my jacket pocket when it should have been back at Pax River in the Air Intelligence Office safe. If I would lose that badge, I would have faced an automatic General Court Marshall. Convicted, I would probably spend a bunch of years on a massive rock pile making little rocks out of big boulders, and my voting days would be over; kaput y'all. This was serious Cold War business and no one in the squadron was immune. There were no "do-overs" nor mulligans. One strike and I would be out, yet Mom wanted me to show her my badge and tell her everything about VAH-7. A talented artist, one look and Mom could have drawn that badge accurately from memory, and would have shown it to every old lady in the whole darn neighborhood.

Mom did not let up for as long as I was at home. Although I enjoyed being there with my family and friends, in desperation I left Wichita a day early because I could not deal with the constant Third Degree all day every day. After I arrived at the Washington, D.C. airport, I went downtown to catch a Grey Hound bus back to Pax River. As I frittered away an hour before that bus was scheduled to leave, I went next door to a fairly large model shop just to look around.

My Dad was a talented model builder when we were kids. He loved to produce as much detail in a model as he possibly could, so I learned to appreciate well-made, highly detailed models of airplanes and ships. That's why I was drawn to that shop's big front window that faced a main street of Washington, D.C., which was possibly the spy capital of the free world at that time. There I saw a beautifully detailed, one-of-a-kind, solid-wood model of the AJ-2 Savage bomber with at least a 30-inch wing span and accurate details up the grommet.

Not only that, but on a large brass plate with bold black letters that must have been at least half an inch tall was written: "AJ-2 SAVAGE—THE NAVY'S ATOM BOMBER."

Give me a break.

5. SNARKY PERSONNEL POGUE'S SILLY GAMES BACKFIRE.

When getting ready to fly the Atlantic from NAS Patuxent River, Maryland to Port Lyautey, French Morocco, a base Personal pogue had me fill out a form stating who I wanted to notify in the event that we would splash in the ocean and became fish food. They wanted the names of my next-of-kin as well as who should get my $10,000 death benefits. But since they worded that form like they did, and neither my Mom nor any other relatives of mine owned an amphibious airplane to come rescue me out of the storm-swept Atlantic Ocean, I wrote: "Please notify Navy Air-Sea Rescue."

Years later, somebody wrote that up for Readers' Digest Magazine and made a few bucks off me, or was that just the "great minds" thing?

The same Personnel twit had given me a bad time earlier when he was picking nits about something trivial that did not add up in my personnel file because that file was not intended to add up accurately in some ways. But then, when I discovered all of the paperwork that he had to do every time that I changed my beneficiaries for my $10,000 government death benefit policy and how much he hated doing all of that paperwork, I made a point of stopping by his desk about once each week or so to change my beneficiaries (as was my privilege) by splitting my benefits between at least five or more people to increase his workload quite a bit. In fact, there was one time when I was running out of options that if I had died that week, Taffy Ferman (our family cocker spaniel back in Wichita) would have received about $2,000 of my $10,000 death benefits.

Finally, just before we shoved off for the Mediterranean, as I was walking to lunch in front of the large picture window in front of that personnel pogue's desk, I saw him sitting there looking at me with wide-eyed deer-in-the-headlights hyper excitement. Although I immediately entered his office space through the closest door about 10 feet away, he was nowhere to be seen in that rather large sea of desks and cubicles. I knew that he had to be hiding under a desk somewhere in that big room, but it was lunch time and I was hungry so I did not take the time to track him down and pull him out of his hidey hole.

Now I kind of wish that I had.

I really got a kick out of that final close encounter because after that he and I both knew that I had his number and could have dumped a sizeable workload on him just for the heck of it rather than the original gallingly opposite situation that he had so smugly dumped on me. What goes around comes around, or as my Irish relatives would say: "Would you mind putting your hat on so I can knock it off yah?

IV. VAH-7 AT THE POINT OF THE SPEAR

1. ESCARGOT ALA BANG, BANG KABOOM

Six months before nearly becoming road kill in the western slums of Istanbul, Turkey, I had just arrived at the French-controlled, U.S. Marine-protected airbase near Port Lyautey, French Morocco. Our 110-man, three AJ-2 atom bomber detachment was preparing to deploy aboard the USS Lake Champlain, CVA-39 (figure 11); a World War II, Essex Class, straight deck, Navy aircraft carrier that was operating in the vicinity of the west coast of Italy at that time.

Since Port Lyautey is fairly close to Rabat, and chances were fairly strong that I might never pass by that way again, I took a local taxi to that exotic French/Muslim city for a quiet day off before what promised to be dangerous, stressful flight operations around the Mediterranean Sea and the countries—both friendly and unfriendly—that surround that clear, blue body of water.

I had not been in Rabat even long enough to sample the local pop skull when I strolled past a cheerful, apparently happy-go-lucky former WW II Wehrmacht (i.e., German regular army) soldier, "Jerry (how appropriate!) Smyth," who was at that time an enlisted rifleman in the French Foreign Legion. For some reason or

Figure 11. USS Lake Champlain CVA-39

other, I said something innocuous like "good afternoon" to Jerry in passing, he said something humorous to me, and after a bit of light banter he graciously invited me to join him over a nearly full jug of cognac at an outdoor café near the middle of downtown Rabat. As I often mentioned in those days, I can resist almost anything except temptation and free adult drinks.

That jovial, seemingly very likeable fellow—although apparently a former Hitler Youth (his age was about right for that) and per chance a former Nazi culprit hiding in plain sight from the aftermath of the Nurnberg trials—Jerry did his best to cajole me into eating a plateful of fat, shelled, wine-soaked, vile-looking, giant snails and washing them down with cognac shooters as if that was the most delightful and enjoyable light lunch possible on such a fine sunny day.

Of course, I didn't know boo doodley about wine-soaked snails. However, I did know that first I had to slug down a heck of a lot of that cognac before I could ever hope to choke down even one of those slimy darned snails without barfing it right back up again. So I had a few more shots of cognac with Jerry while he and I traded jokes, and Jerry regaled me with hilarious stories about the humorous habits of the beautiful but deadly little brown people in North Vietnam.

Surprisingly, I was holding up my end of the conversation by converting old jokes about Oklahoma A&M Aggies to Italian jokes, which got over amazingly well. However, just as I had finally gotten around to gagging down the first slippery, fat blob of a whole slimy snail that was about the size of my thumb, what must have been a hand grenade exploded unseen around the street corner, followed by heavy rifle and machinegun fire, yelling, screaming, crying and more explosions suddenly erupting in a fierce battle between Arab rebels and French troops immediately around the corner but still unseen. That intense firefight was raging just barely obscured by the corner of the building at which Jerry and I were sitting and no more than 40 or 50 feet away. That was much too darned close for comfort as stray bullets and shards from the building's facade ricocheted off the road close beside our table.

Recess was over. Jerry stood up languidly as if stretching every muscle in his body, emptied his shot glass of cognac in a single gulp, slid the two-thirds-full bottle of cognac across the table to me as he bid me adieu and, faithful to his oath to his latest bosses, he picked up his rifle, shrugged as if to say "here we go again," and disappeared around the corner of that building to join in the pitched battle raging too damned close for comfort.

Since I did not have a dog in that fight, I grabbed the bottle of cognac, slid a five-franc tip for the Arab waiter under Jerry's cognac glass, and then cut out in the opposite direction running flat out to put as many buildings between me and the barrages of flying ammunition and shrapnel that were kicking up chunks of cobble stones in the streets too damn close to my right. Welcome to Rabat, French Morocco.

As I recall, a wise old rummy once said: "Never mess with another man's fire fight when there's free cognac on the line."

Sometimes I think about ol' Jerry, the affable former Hitler Youth, Wehrmacht survivor, self-described connoisseur and street-corner bon vivant. I wonder if that cognac and lunch of marinated giant snails was his last meal on God's green earth, or if he heard the evening call for prayer from deep within the comforts of his favorite bordello.

I have to admit that I have never eaten escargot since then, and don't plan to start again now. However, I cannot say the same for the pure satisfaction of free cognac.

2. RABAT'S KASBAH AFTER DARK

My new friend, Stan "big Swig" Swigonski joined the U.S. Navy in 1936 and had been a Navy enlisted air-crewman ever since. A tall, dark, good-looking professional sailor and natural leader, Swig was a fine example for all enlisted airmen. He stood out from the crowd in so many ways. Everyone who knew him liked and respected big Swig.

Serving his last overseas deployment before his retirement after 20 years of active duty, Swig had been to the Mediterranean many times and knew a lot of the local Arab businessmen and high mucky mucks in Rabat. When they learned that Swig was back in town, they threw a party for him at a private home in the Kasbah; the native inner city which was surrounded by ancient mud ramparts that still showed damage from the first American battle in North Africa back in WW II. However, inside the battle-scarred outer walls, the homes were pristine, airy, bright, sumptuous and very welcoming.

Despite the bloody ambush in Rabat just two days before, I decided to accept Swig's invitation to join him, and we had a heck of a good time that evening for the most part. Swig and I met a lot of extremely hospitable and friendly local Muslim people who were quite adept at throwing a really enjoyable party without any alcohol whatsoever. Aaaa-danged-mazing! The music ranged from whispering reed thin and soothing to something like North African Holy Rollers on steroids.

Surprisingly, I discovered that I really liked sipping their mint tea, nibbling on various fruits, eating open-faced sandwich-like thingys on fresh flat bread that were made with I don't know what kind of meat (but it was very good), and telling nice people a few sea stories. Of course, that was mostly in pantomime because I only knew a few non-cuss words of their language, and all of those were inappropriate for that occasion.

Actually, I seemed to be a big hit with the jovial but somewhat formal crowd when I tried to describe American geography to them in pantomime. I even took a hit on a water pipe; an honor that could not be refused, although I certainly thought about that. All in all, a good time was had by all even though I could not have remembered a single name the next day if that would have guaranteed world peace. "Yes ma'am" and "No sir" worked just fine for me. As Swig reminded me, the Qur'an forbids the use of nicknames, which otherwise I would have used for convenience. An Arab's name is his honor, and a wise man would not fool around with an Arab's honor; not if he wanted to see the sunrise the next morning.

Sometime around midnight, Swig and I said our goodbyes to my new friends, shook hands with every male in the house, left the party and headed back to the base when I discovered the obvious. There were no street lights on the narrow, circuitous, cobblestone lanes of the Kasbah. Not one. There were darned few feeble sparks of light from any of the abutted lines of homes that formed a solid wall on both sides of the many winding and intersecting lanes. Under a minimal moon and broken cumulous clouds racing overhead, forbidding dark shadows lurked along the various lanes from the crude stone gutters to the flat rooftops. Occasionally, those dark shadows moved silently and menacingly as we passed.

So I began a running conversation with Swig, talking loud enough in an exaggerated southern Kansas/semi-hillbilly accent so that anyone, especially black robed folks (French hating Berbers?) scattered among the dark shadows, would know that we were loudmouthed Americans and not French fops to be murdered. I actually said: "By golly Jethroe, we sure could put a bodacious heap of wheat in that there silo."

We had no doubt that if we were mistaken for Frenchmen, we would not live to see the sun rise. Although we had a really great, memorable grand time that night, I do not have the nerve to go back to the Kasbah today. Many things have changed since then, and I would not want to push my luck that far again. My momma did not raise any fools, although there were times when I was momentarily fairly darned sure that she had.

3. AJ-2 SAVAGE ATOM BOMBER REDUX

The AJ-2 Savage bomber, with its two reciprocating R2800 radial-engines under the wings and one J-51 turbojet engine aft in the tail assembly, was the Navy's only aircraft carrier-based atomic bomber.

Every other atom-bomb delivery system hyped by the Navy and Marines was just another strawman diversion to fool the Iron Curtain bad guys. This aircraft was a cold-war Top Secret weapon system that the Navy tried to hide by flying lots of high-publicity air-to-air refueling missions such as John Glenn's cross-country speed record using a probe-and-drogue air-to-air hookup dangling behind the drop tank that was temporarily mounted inside the AJ's large bomb bay.

However, some hide-bound bureaucratic dim bulbs in La La Land D. C.—in their too-often questionable wisdom—designated the squadron VAH-7. Since just about everyone including the frigging Soviets knew that the "V" meant "fixed wing aircraft," the "A" meant "attack," and the "H" meant "heavy;" which all together equated to atom bombers and not air-to-air refueling. We weren't fooling anyone that counted, and that was our own danged fault. The only data obfuscated was that we only had a few VAH squadrons while the Navy's numbering system inferred that we had many more. Every little bit counted, I guess, when gambling against the stacked deck of the Soviet air defense squadrons that were packed with the new MiG-15 jet fighters (figure 12) which were arguably the best jet fighter/interceptor war planes in the world at that time.

Figure 12 Soviet MIG-15 Fighter Aircraft

4. VAH-7 DIRTY LITTLE SECRET

The dirty little secret was that the VAH squadrons had been disasters from Day One. The AJ-2 bomber was the biggest aircraft ever operated off an Essex-class aircraft carrier, and their graying senior-command multi-engine pilots—due to regulations about who was qualified to fly hither and yon with atomic bombs stuffed in their bomb bays—generally had not played aircraft-carrier launch and tail-hook landing games since qualifying many years before when they were NavCads flying little bitty two-seater training planes before and during WW II.

The lumbering AJ's were awkward and even dangerous in an aircraft carrier's low-level, racetrack, landing pattern, which was often crammed full with much faster, more nimble aircraft.

Furthermore, the AJ pilots wanted a much longer straight-in pattern on final approach to the carrier, but the Navy brass in their wisdom said: "No sale. Leave that tradition alone." I understood that several AJ air crews were lost in carrier takeoff and landing operations, or practicing for those hairy operations.

The enlisted air crews were disgruntled because they had a hard time getting promoted within their MOSs—Military Occupational Specialties: e.g., electrical twiggets, metal benders, grease monkeys, bosons, etc.—since most if not all of their duty time was spent flying or in briefings and flight preparations rather than improving their proficiencies within their official MOS job descriptions. In fact, I understood that the Navy did not have an MOS for enlisted flight crew members at that time, although they had been an essential element in naval aviation since the late 1930s. However, I am not absolutely certain on that count and never bothered to check it out because that did not mean zilch to me. My retirement rank was already established; at least that was what I was promised.

Furthermore, the morale of the maintenance personnel in our detachment was bloody awful due to their unusually too-long and too-hectic working conditions, and somewhat exacerbated by openly elitist senior officer ring-knockers from east coast university icons like Annapolis, Harvard, Yale, etc., as well as mui-entitled playboy Ivy League fraternity pogues. I remember late one night in our Ready Room on the Lake Champlain aircraft carrier when a group of our officers thought that they were alone. At that time, one of our senior officers lectured a less senior officer by confiding that all of his enlisted men—every one of those overworked lads who were making him look real good as well as keeping him alive—were "the scum of the earth" who would "steal the fillings out of your teeth if they could."

About that time, our incoming mail was often addressed to "VAH-7 SUX" by unwitting family members back in the states. They were only repeating the return addresses furnished them by their loved ones who were enlisted in squadron VAH-7.

5. MEDITERRANEAN MUSTACHE MYSTIQUE

In the countries around the Mediterranean Sea, an adult male was not considered to be a real man until he could sport a mature (i.e., thick, bushy) mustache. So what the heck, as soon as we got there, darned near every guy in the squadron began growing a mustache. After a couple of weeks at sea, we were all beginning to look fairly decent mustache wise, and we enjoyed the new look almost regardless of the accompanying facial itches. However, our squadron commander back at Port Lyautey, Navy Captain (we called him "Elmer Fudd" because of an amazing similarity) was unable to grow a presentable mustache. Apparently, his looked thin and scraggly like a scruffy Fu Manchu, so he eventually shaved it off. To each his own, right?

Yeah, you bet. However, fairly quickly the word came trickling down from squadron headquarters in Port Lyautey that although mustaches were certainly not verbotten, they were not the right image for those who hungered for promotions and more pay in our VAH-7 squadron. As family men with dependents galore, almost immediately every officer except my buddy Lt. Weigle, a bombardier/navigator, fell in line one-by-one, trimmed back their mustaches, and then eventually caved in and shaved them off.

Since I was not a ring knocker nor the least bit interested in maintaining a squeaky clean proficiency report, I enjoyed the latitude to ignore the whole pissing contest and continued growing my mustache as little by little almost the entire shipboard squadron became clean shaven.

Besides that, I discovered that mustaches can get awfully itchy. At about half way through the Med tour, I had had about enough of that doggone irritation under my nose and decided to cut my mustache off right after my last debriefing and quick-look mission report were finished for that evening. I had just gotten up from my leather easy chair with folding work table in the ready room and was reaching for the door handle to head for the head (i.e., bathroom) to shave off my mui bothersome soup strainer when our detachment C.O. came bursting through the door like a bull in a china shop and exclaimed excitedly: "Hey Dave. You ought to see Lt. Weigle. He just shaved off his mustache, and he looks great!"

Right there, right then, on that very spot, I vowed to myself to keep that itchy darned irritating mustache until I would be discharged back in the States. Despite everything to the contrary as well as the Personnel pogue's pressure a'plenty, I stuck to my guns and put up with the itching to the dismay of every officer in the detachment.

Ooooooooh-rahhh. Semper fi.

6. SCURVY A'PLENTY IN 1955

Amazingly, we had scurvy—shades of the Middle Ages you might say—on the USS Lake Champlain, CVA-39 in the summer of 1955. Who'da thunk it? Although the Lake Champ and the other aircraft carrier received the exact same provisions, measure for measure from the one food provisioning ship in the Med, somehow the guys on every other ship of the Sixth Fleet must have been eating all of their veggies to stay healthy. However, a lot of our guys on the Lake Champ were getting ugly blotches on their chests from a lack of veggies and their essential doses of vitamins.

Besides the shoulder patch's or baseball hats with each ship's logo, anyone could always tell who were from the Lake Champ because when we hit a decent liberty port, the guys from the other ships would stampede into town to chase exotic women and chug down frosty adult beverages galore. Our guys, however, would first zero in on the nearest restaurant and eat them out of vegetables and salads. Then our guys would chase exotic women and frosty adult beverages galore.

Fortunately, the flight mess always had tomato or orange juice on hand, so I cannot tell you what scurvy feels like. But take my word for it, scurvy looks bloody awful.

7. HAPPINESS IS A PUSHCART FULL OF CHERRY BOMB FIRECRACKERS.

Kind of, sort of disguised in civilian clothes, I was sitting solo under a beach-type umbrella enjoying a few adult beverages on the patio of an open-air bar in Palma, Majorca. This bar was on the top of a fairly steep hill overlooking an exclusive bar that apparently catered solely to a gaggle of uniformly large, loud mouthed, openly gay, British homosexuals. As if it was their own esoteric uniform, almost all of those guys seemed to be dressed in heavy and expensive tweed sport jackets with pinched waists and Swiss mountain hats featuring various bird plumes despite the semi-tropical climate of the Mediterranean Sea in mid July. Go figure.

As expected, words were exchanged between the U.S. Navy sailors on liberty and the fern bar Brits, who seemed to be not only loud and obnoxious, but very proud of themselves. Soon, push came to shove, shove led to the gathering of the various clans, and all hell was about to explode when the Brits counted noses and came up short by a lot. So they took refuge inside their fern bar where the management forbade entrance to anyone not wearing one of those silly darned Swiss mountain hats as well as the heavy sport jackets nipped at the waist. I thought they looked silly, but my pal Frank (i.e., Si) Simonsen bought one and liked it a lot although Si was definitely not one of "those guys."

Wouldn't you know that right away an enterprising local business man rolled out an enormous two-wheel pushcart piled high with big red cherry-bomb fire crackers. Bargains at the local equivalent of less than 10 cents each, our sailors bought them by the bucket full and then tossed those loud little boogers in rain-like volleys into the front door of that fern bar hangout.

Panicked, the bar owner called the Palma police, who never showed up, and the U.S. Navy Shore Patrol, which sent a five-man unit led by a young, officious, twerp of an ensign who still had the quartermaster creases in his new dress uniform. Obviously, even from afar, he was not the right man for the job. Badly outnumbered, the entire SP unit and their fearless leader were unceremoniously tossed into the clear, warm waters of the beautiful round harbor of Palma as the rioting sailors laughed a lot and continued their jovial bombardment of the fern bar while I enjoyed the show and had a few more frosty adult beverages from my primo observation table maybe 30 feet above the fray.

Eventually, all good things come to an end and, finally, after what seemed to be about an hour of unbridled revelry, the 6th Fleet sent a Marine MP detachment ashore. Those guys broke up the riot, pointedly ignored the now-hysterical Brits wailing bloody murder from inside their bar, directed our sailors to move along like gentlemen, then returned to their other shore duties in good order.

As always, I was proud to be a Marine. In fact, I gave them a round of spontaneous applause from my cigarette butt/dead-soldier bottle strewn table high above the fray.

8. CUTE CAIO BELLA STOWAWAY AT SEA

One evening about two days out at sea from Genoa, I was going to the ship's aft shower room wearing only a large beach towel and flip flops when suddenly a tall, statuesque Italian beauty wearing only a luxurious hotel towel and a big smile passed me head-on in an otherwise empty passageway. To paraphrase Rudyard Kipling's *Gunga Din*: "The uniform she wore was nothing much before, and little less than half of that behind."

We were about five decks down from the then-active flight deck on the USS Lake Champlain and, if you will recall, no women were serving on-board U.S. aircraft carriers back in 1955. However, I guaran-danged-tee you that young lady was a wondrous sight to behold. I knew that she must be the private property of some jet-jockey sugar daddy who probably snuck her onboard and would not be inclined to share her companionship. So I said a cheery "Ciao" right back at her in passing, and then hurried to the head and took a long cold shower.

Sometimes it is best to shut up and let the chips fall where they may. To quote the much-repeated near-mantra of German Sgt. Schultz on the *Hogan's Heroes* TV show: "I know NOTHING. I saw NOTHING!"

By the way, after that first sighting, none of us ever saw or heard about that young lady again.

9. TOP SECRET INFORMATION; NOT FUN AND GAMES

One Thursday around noon, "Big Swig" Swigonski and I went ashore in Naples for a much deserved night on the town after a long and hectic cruise at sea. Our Sixth Fleet had been tracking two Russian submarines that had been tracking us: one sub for the USS Lake Champlain Battle Group and the other sub for the USS Ticonderoga Battle Group. We knew those Ruskies were out there because we had sonar data on them, and even occasional radar contacts in the dark of night when they would occasionally surface to take a break and clean their air below decks.

In addition to all of the ASW (i.e., anti-submarine warfare) goodies on our destroyer escort ships, we also had ASW-equipped AD Skyraider hunter/killer aircraft teams working in pairs, and P2V recon aircraft in the air around the clock trying to trap a sub in a corner for a clear Cold War simulated victory. However, we could not get a clear simulated "kill" on them as if this was a real wartime battle instead of what was essentially a rather tense training operation for both sides of the Iron Curtain 24/7. Those Ruskies were good at what they did, and they were a clear and present danger if World War III should suddenly erupt. We really needed to blow some smoke up their fannies just to keep them honest.

Swig and I were both exhausted from too many 16-hour days for several weeks in a row, so we were looking for a big steak dinner with all of the trimmings, and some adult beverages to get our afternoon jump-started on the right note. So we hailed a cab to get away from the harbor area, which still had bomb damage from WW II, and were picked up by one of the large, fat, obnoxious cab-driver/pimps who lurked around the main dock when the U.S. fleet was in town. Most of them—including this old lech—were always trying to rent their daughters, wives, sisters and other female relatives to any guy who had the ready cash. The common denominator: "Shee ees a veerjin. Shee ees az phurr az nuu snooo." At least that was their story and they stuck with it although almost everyone knew better.

As we drove toward the nearest decent restaurant in the better rebuilt heart of downtown Naples, just for conversation's sake since we didn't want to play house with his female relatives, the cabby asked if the two of us from the Lake Champ would be ashore again on Saturday or Sunday. We told him no; he could take the day off because our battle group would be back at sea at that time.

Immediately, the cabby laughed uproariously and then pointedly corrected me. He said with confident certainty that the Lake Champ would leave Naples the next day—which apparently everyone in Naples knew—on Friday, but would be back at Naples the following day on Saturday.

I was absolutely flabbergasted. That was Top-Secret information. The cab driver was absolutely right, although only about 20 or so people in our entire battle group knew about that tactical ruse. While ridiculing the whole idea, I asked him where he got such "crappy gossip." Argumentative to a fault—he was one of those obnoxious people who had to be competitively right in every instance—the cabby said that since driving a cab was one of his many businesses, he had to know when which NATO fleet elements would arrive in Naples, and when they would leave Naples. He bragged that he had his contacts, but he would not say who. I gave him a hard time, but he would not back off, and even offered to put some fairly big money down on that sure bet.

So much for my big night on the town. As soon as that cab dropped us off, I made a lame excuse to Swig, who then took off to renew old acquaintances from several previous cruises, and I hailed another cab and returned to the ship where I reported our conversation with that cabby to Naval Intelligence, and also gave them specific information to identify that big mouthed crud and his cab. I figured that one way or another, he was toast. However, our tactical ruse was cast in concrete, so we muddled through with it regardless.

Our carrier group planned to head south through the very shallow channel of the Mycenae Strait between the toe of Italy and Sicily. That would force the shadowing Russian sub—if it had any hope of keeping in contact with us—to nearly surface in that unusually shallow ship channel, and thus be fully visible to our ASW air elements and vulnerable to our fast-moving destroyer escorts who would play "tag, you're it" with the Russians. We would be all over that sub like ducks on June bugs, and the Russian Naval big wigs would have to change their tactics if WW III would break out the next day.

But surprise, surprise, that sub took a right turn at Sicily, went around that large island counterclockwise, and met us in deep water as we came back around the island clockwise on our way back to Naples. Tag, we were it again.

We just hated it when those Bolshevik wise guys did that.

When Si and I went ashore in Naples that Saturday evening, that same fat, sleazy, pimp cab driver was still infecting the dock area, and cheerfully waved at me in victorious jubilation as he drove by us with a cab full of horny sailors. Later, I learned that exactly the same thing happened regularly in Japan. The local merchants and hookers knew the ships' supposedly classified schedules as well as the U.S. Navy did. Who'da thunk it?

Me, that's who. Apparently, some S.O.B. in an American uniform was selling classified information to the cab drivers, pimps, and other merchants in Naples. Whoever that S.O.B. was, I hoped that somebody would stick a shiv in his gut once and then walk around him twice.

10. SALTY OLD CHIEF BOSUN MATE'S GAFF

Another old-salt Navy guy was the Chief Bosun's Mate on the USS Lake Champlain. This grizzled, old, self-styled "Sea Daddy" announced all of the events on the ship over the PA system, and his uber bored and salty voice was often heard announcing such events as: "This...is...a... drill. This...is...a... drill. There...is...a...fire...at...bulkhead... (whatever). All...hands ...man...your...fire stations."

Then, one afternoon, one of our F9F fighter planes (figure 13) landed short of the flight deck right smack dab in the spud locker at the ship's fantail, blew up, and the whole aft end of the Lake Champ was ablaze. At that moment, that old salt Chief Bosun's Mate blew his entire image as he shouted into the PA system: "Fireinthefantail! Fireinthefantail! NO SHIT!"

Figure 13. F9F Fighter Aircraft

11. "UNTIL THE REAL THING COMES ALONG, CHA, CHA, CHA."

The Isle of Rhodes is a very pretty place, and a fascinating port to visit. The little towns and villas plastered on the steep sides of precipitous mountains, the white and blue painted buildings gleaming brightly against the deep blue water of the ancient volcano caldron, the pristine black sand beaches, the ancient Greek fortifications and the picturesque villages with crowded streets no wider than an alley, the quaint bars and bistros with drying octopus tentacles hanging down over the entry doorways like beaded strings; everything about Rhodes was fascinating and exciting. I could not get enough of that beautiful island in the deep blue Mediterranean Sea.

One gorgeous afternoon, Frank Simonsen (we called him "Si"), myself and another air crewman who I'll call Randy for reasons soon to be obvious, were riding our rented single-speed bicycles downhill on an extremely narrow lane in a tiny but crowded village when we asked a pretty lass for directions to someplace or other. Surprisingly, she did not know how to get there (say "what!"), so she asked us to come inside to ask someone else, and that's what we did.

But since this wasn't our first rodeo, we brought our bikes inside too or they would not have been there when we came back out of that house even 30 seconds later. I'm pretty sure that "pretty lass" did not know that we knew better than to leave our bicycles leaning against the walls of that lane because she was surprised when we boldly brought them inside the house with us. Several of us were born at night, but not the preceding night.

The first thing that we noticed was how bright it was inside that house. Apparently every room in that building had a large opening in the roof overhead that could be closed and capped with a heavy wooden storm door during bad weather. The second thing we noticed was that the sultry woman inside was not wearing a whole heck of a lot of clothes when we got there, and what clothes she did wear did not cover much of her nicely tanned body.

Anyway, eee-mediately if not sooner, Randy got the Big Eye for that tantalizingly tanned gal, took her by her hand, and she led him into the nearest room, shut the door and slid the bolt. It all happened so fast that Si and I missed most of the expected negotiations, if there was any of that at all.

However, above that solid door was an open transom, so Si leaned a bike against the door, crawled up on bike's crossbar, peeked into the transom and would have fallen off if he hadn't grabbed the sill. Then he reached for my Bell & Howell 8mm movie camera, and shot my last roll of film without stopping. He would have shot more if I had any more film.

As we later learned, the sunlight streaming down into that room was perfect for amateur photography. The available light could not have been better on a sun-drenched beach as Si and I quietly harmonized on the refrain of that old country classic, to wit: "Well if that isn't love, it will have to do, until the real thing comes along."

Back on the Lake Champ, I pulled a few strings to have that film processed in our photo lab; the one that handles all of our highly classified tactical operations. Fortunately, those lab guys were glad to make an exception. Then we took the film unseen and a projector down to the squadron's enlisted men's bunk room, and setup a stretched white sheet as a movie screen in the tightly packed space between two sets of double-decker bunks. When Randy sat down on the bottom bunk with maybe a dozen guys jammed in and around that very tight space, someone turned off the light, Si turned on the projector and let 'er rip.

Bug eyed, Randy leaned closer to see better, got all excited and yelled: "Hey, look at that. Look at that. Oh my gosh. Oh my gosh." Then there was a brief pause, after which Randy bellowed: "Hey…that's me; that's ME dammit! Dave, you son of a bitch." I was laughing so hard at Randy's reaction that I could not defend myself in those close quarters, and I couldn't even talk to deny his misdirected accusations as he pounded on me the best he could in those tight quarters. Meanwhile, Si, the real culprit of this off-color drama, got off scot free, and had a good laugh at both Randy and me. Someday, when I have nothing else to do, I may get even.

Later, after everyone settling down, we gave Randy the only copy of that film marked "Original—No Copies" by the Photo Lab. No one thought that his sweetie back home would appreciate the humor of that occasion, and no one wanted that prospect hanging over Randy while he was putting his life on the line for God and country with the rest of the air crews. That would have been an unnecessary mell of a hess for Randy to carry in addition to all of the other stresses of our trade. VAH-7 air crewmen kid around sometimes, but always stick together.

12. PHOTO BANSHEE HOT SHOTS

Photo Banshee Squadron, VF-11, the Red Rippers, flew supposedly obsolete fighter planes that were yet another Cold War surprise for "Uncle Joe" Stalin and his motley minions. At that time, those twin-jet, single pilot, straight wing rather than swept wing old post-WW II Banshee fighter planes were already outdated and could have been sold as scrap. However, these deceptive-looking old aircraft had been stripped of all of their weapons and their heavy armor plating. Then, their twin engines were replaced with two of the biggest, baddest jet engines of that time and were supercharged with afterburners that were still at least Secret if not Top Secret.

Although they must have looked like easy prey to the sleek Russian MiG-15s at first glance, those Banshees were the hotrods of the sky. Friend or foe, nobody could catch them in straight and level flight. Nobody. Naturally, the VF-11 pilots began to believe that they were very special, and they missed few chances to show off to anyone just how special they really were. I don't know how many Photo Banshee squadrons were in the Navy's bag of tricks at that time, but there had to be at least two, or possibly more.

With their two banks of top-of-the-line, high-altitude, aerial cameras—one bank on the side and one on the bottom of the light-weight, custom nose section—these hotshot aerial cowboys flew over Iron Curtain countries to take excellent photographs with their side-mounted cameras and/or collect radar mapping data. When they were invariably chased by the Soviets' fastest hot-shot fighters, the MiG-15s, those Banshees would turn around 180 degrees, firewall those great honking engines, kick in their super-dooper afterburners and leave the bad guys bumfoozled far behind them while the Banshees took more reels of photographs with their bottom-mounted banks of cameras while on their pre-planned flight paths out of those countries' air spaces.

These hotshots were notorious for taking chances, playing death-defying yet ultimately fun games, and breaking standard Navy regulations and flight rules hither and yon. It is possible that these Red Ripper guys would make even Pappy Boyington's Black Sheep hotshots from WW II look like choir boys. If they didn't, it wasn't for lack of trying.

In fact, one of our VF-11 photo Banshees flew an unauthorized, "practice," extra-low, high-speed, port-to-starboard pass over the stern of the anchored USS Lake Champlain (figure 14) while Generalissimo Franco, the President of Spain, was being honored at a formal ceremony on the bow of the Lake Champ. The Banshee pilot's lame excuse: he was checking out some maintenance performed at Port Lyautey and his radio wasn't working, so he did not know that President Franco was onboard even on such a severe clear day.

Furthermore, somehow he did not notice the massive gaggle of massed military brass, VIPs and brass band gathered at the bow of the Lake Champ at anchor. Oh heck no, that darn-well works for me. But did it work for our admiral? I doubt it.

Ironically, the missions of both squadrons occupying Ready Room One involved quite a bit of flying over Soviet Iron Curtain countries. That additional stress came with the already stressful issues of aircraft carrier operations. Every aviator in that ready room knew that quite a few U.S. military aircraft had flown intentionally or unintentionally into Soviet air space and were never seen again.

From former Russian political prisoners who served their sentences and were released from Russian prisons in Siberian gulags, the Russians were known to have American prisoners from WW II and the Korean War, as well as pilots and crews from the Cold War in their Siberian gulags. But the Soviets stonewalled all inquiries about U.S. prisoners (i.e., no names, ranks nor serial numbers) except for Francis Gary Powers of U2 fame who did not take his get-out-of-jail-forever pill before his capture and was paraded before world-wide TV and other reporters so that the Soviets could not deny that he was still alive.

Figure 14. VF-11 Banshee Buzzing Anchored USS Lake Champlain

Although they were all aware of the horrendous consequences awaiting them if shot down behind the Soviet Iron Curtain, the VF-11 photo Banshee pilots as well as our VAH-7 pilots and crewmen did not know the full magnitude of the intimidating threat. They knew the consequences of being shot down behind the Iron Curtain and they knew that a number of our aircraft had been shot down. However, very few knew that the United States lost more than 152 military aircraft and crews behind the Iron Curtain during just Cold War activities, and many of those aircraft were multi-engine aircraft that had fairly large crews.

There are not enough obscene cuss words in the English language to properly condemn those barbaric Soviet bastards for throwing our military airmen into their deplorable prisons for life with no hope of ever being released because there was no record of them being captured or even being alive. Yet on any given day, the pilots and crews of Ready Room One put their lives and their futures on the line to keep the United States prepared, strong and free.

I am proud and honored to have served at NAS Moffett Field with the men of the 1st and 5th Marine Regiments of the 1st Marine Division which, during the "Frozen Chosin Reservoir" campaign in North Korea, were surrounded by three Chinese communist (ChiCom) divisions. However, that single Marine division decimated all three ChiCom divisions so that they were no longer viable fighting units.

In fact, the remaining seven invading ChiCom divisions were then instructed by their high command to avoid the "yellow legs" (i.e., the 1st Marine Division who were wearing dull yellowish puttees) and to "attack only the American Army." When he heard that, Colonel Chesty Fuller commanded his Marines to take off their puttees so that the ChiCom soldiers could not tell Marines from Army forces. Chesty came to Korea to fight and win, not to observe from the sidelines.

I don't mind saying that I am equally proud and honored to have served with the men of VAH-7. Their presence in the Mediterranean Theatre and the presence of all of the Navy heavy attack (i.e., atomic bomber) squadrons was a definite deterrent to World War III. Those brave men were the real, unsung heroes of the Cold War. They did their duty despite horrendous potential consequences. God bless 'em all.

13. HOLY HAL'S COMEUPPANCE

One of the older pilots in VF-11 was a very religious guy—we called him Holy Hal—who refused to go ashore with his squadron mates in the magnificent, historic ports of Greece, Turkey, Spain, France, Italy, Lebanon, et al. because of all the sin and debauchery that he was sure was lurking there. That probably would have been okay with everyone in the ready room, except that Holy Hal also insisted on lecturing anyone and everyone who went ashore (i.e., darned near everybody else) about the debauchery and sin rampant in those beautiful liberty ports. He let us all know in no uncertain terms that we were therefore awful, bad-nasty sinners who were doomed to hellfire, brimstone and eternal damnation because we went ashore rather than stay aboard the Lake Champ with him. Do I hear an "Aaa-men" from the rear with the gear?

Finally, toward the end of VF-11's Mediterranean cruise, that pilot's wife traveled all the way from the USA to Italy, rented a beautiful villa in the hills above Naples so that old boy finally went ashore, but only to be with his dear wife. That was sooo sweet, and we were happy for him. Really, we were incredibly happy to see him finally get the heck off the Lake Champ and out of Ready Room One for a while.

However, the story gets better because about a week after that fine, upstanding officer and gentleman finally returned from his dear wife's Italian love nest, we were far out to sea when, according to a ship's corpsman, that semi-saintly good example for all of us dastardly sinners to emulate had to check himself in at the sickbay with a brand new dose of VD, which he had apparently caught from someone on shore. Since everyone in both squadrons was so darned weary of his sanctimonious lectures, I doubt if there were many onboard the Lake Champ who did not know about the sudden misfortune of the Red Ripper's holier-than-thou pilot.

Navy corpsmen are the good guys. They don't tell fibs, do they?

14. NASTY GENOA WATERFRONT NEIGHBORHOOD

Si and I were diddy bopping down a narrow alley on the waterfront in Genoa, Italy one morning when a couple of Italians slicky boys—think young adult street yahoos—echoed a fairly decent imitation of my just unleashed Arapaho War Cry that reverberated off the ancient brick walls and curled the toes of many a late sleeper. That was good enough for openers, so they joined up with us and we had a hilarious howling contest as we continued down the dingy alley in search of Christopher Columbus' still-standing, childhood home.

As we continued deeper into that ancient waterfront neighborhood, a couple of their friends joined us, and then a couple more, followed by a couple more until there were eight of them and just the two of us. At that point, those homeboys dropped their good guys ruse, turned hostile on us, and tried to strong-arm rob both of us just because their numbers favored them by a heck of a lot.

With my adrenaline suddenly pumping like a fire hose, everything slowed down a notch or two as I hit a couple of them hard enough to break their beaks so that those two pukes sat down on the cobblestones crying. They were done for the day. However, that free-for-all was still in doubt since they still had a six-to-two advantage, which was not good, especially when we were isolated on their turf.

Although Si always was a cool head, a top-notch AJ air crewman, and a dedicated Navy warrior, I didn't believe that he could fistfight his way out of a wet paper sack. With our backs against a moldy old warehouse wall and Si's prescription sunglasses lying shattered on the cobblestones, Si began myopically swinging his fists wildly like a windmill and doing surprisingly well at it. That seemed to momentarily baffle the slicky boys that were coming after him.

When they hesitated a moment to regroup, Si and I hooked 'em out of there through an even narrower alley (about four feet wide) for about two blocks to a main street with the six enraged slicky boys hot on our heels. They wanted vengeance for their two buddies' bloody broken noses and their loss of what they thought would be an easy payday.

At the end of that alley at a main street, we turned on our pursuers who did not want to pop out of that narrow alley one at a time, especially with the Italian street cops too close for their comfort. Aside from Si's broken glasses, we kind of, sort of won that one, and if we had the sense that God gave a rubber duck, we should never return to that lousy slum neighborhood again.

But I did anyway. The very next day Si had the duty, so Randy and I went back to find Christopher Columbus' house and a "really great" bar somewhere in that same general area that catered to American military personnel who had their pockets full of extra "whipout" cash to play with. And once again, Randy and I ran into a couple of young

Italian bucks who could not speak any more English that we could speak Italian. As long as there was only two of them, everything was copacetic because unlike Si, Randy was a brawler who could kick Italian butts at any and all opportunities. In the field, Randy would have made a darned good Marine.

So once again, we communicated with the Italians by sign language. Since it was a warm day in Genoa, Randy and I were looking for some frosty cold drinks to wet our whistles. Just like before, we tried to use hand signals to indicate that we each wanted to drink a couple of icy cold Coca Cokes, preferably mixed with rum or any other adult popskull. We were too darned thirsty to be picky.

No comprendo. So Randy formed the shape of a curvy Coca Cola bottle with both hands in the air, then shook his horizontal hands vertically to indicate a mixed drink. Try that sometime. When miming with just your hands and smiling a lot, a Coke bottle held horizontally and shaken vertically could easily be mistaken for something else. And yeah, those guys seemed to understand that international symbol for a cold Coca Cola mixed drink very well. At least, we thought they did.

As we were walking across a very old and nearly deserted neighborhood square, we ran into a couple of Italian cops on patrol, who had a brief conversation with our slicky boy guides. Then they proceeded to lead us into a shabby looking four-story warehouse-like building that I would have avoided like the plague if not for the company and encouragement of the local cops.

After climbing some dark and dingy stairs up three stories, we were verified by the police to a beady eyed, extremely serious woman behind a sliding peep hole in a heavy duty door, then ceremoniously admitted into an absolutely luxurious room with huge, bright chandeliers, mirrored walls and fine leather divans lining the walls around that room. As I rubber-necked around that lavish room to take it all in, basically blown away by the overall elegance of the place, a gaggle of six or eight young gals came in from an adjoining room to welcome Randy and I, both cops, and the two slicky boys with mui enthusiasm. Every one of those gals wore essentially the same thing; a scanty Greek toga-like getup and not much else. I swear, several of those gals could have been centerfolds for Playboy magazine.

"Damn," I thought. "This sure is one great bar. I sure hope they have rum and Coca Cola and plenty of ice cubes."

But surprise, surprise, that was not a bar at all, and the situation rapidly segued directly into the kind of fantasy mob scene that most teenaged boys only dream about. Although blown away by the whole concept, for some inexplicable reason, I eee-mediately remembered how Randy had chided me that morning for always getting him into some kind of trouble while on liberty. Naturally, I thought it was the other way around.

In fact, I really enjoyed directing each gal who tried to snuggle up with me to go over and join the festivities swirling around Randy, the two cops and our original tour guides. In no time at all, Randy was completely overwhelmed by a gaggle of giggling, exciting, competitive young Italian gals who could have easily doubled as sorority sisters from Central Casting.

Since those beautiful, exotic gals were professional hookers and I did not want to do something fun for a few minutes that could ruin my life forever, I took a bow and quietly slipped out the door and down the stairs to the battered old square to wait for Randy to re-appear so that I could set him straight on who gets who in trouble while on liberty.

So I waited and waited and waited a heck of a long time until Randy finally came outside grinning like a Cheshire cat and covered with lick stick and hickies. Naturally curious after waiting all of that time, I asked him what took him so darned long. His answer then and ever since then has always been: "Davy, 'ol pal, you will never, never know."

That reminds me. Do you remember the large model of the AJ-2 bomber in the front window of the hobby shop in Washington, DC; the one with the eight-inch-wide brass plate that read: "AJ-2 Savage: the U.S. Navy's Atom Bomber?" That was one of many security faux pas since that information was supposed to be Top Secret as the Navy continued to stubbornly insist on the official ruse that VAH-7 was an air-to-air refueling squadron. Again and again, we were reminded how shallow and foolish that sham really was.

For example, on the fourth and last day of our visit at Genoa, we held an open house on the USS Lake Champ and invited anybody and everybody in the area to come aboard by Navy liberty launches, meet our guys, take a gander at our many displays, and generally have a good time. As the number two guy in our VAH-7 Air Intelligence office, I was volunteered to show one of our AJ-2 "air-to-air refueling" aircraft and answer questions from our visitors. What could go wrong?

How about darn near everything?

After a few hours of unclassified show-and-tell with curious groups of visitors, as the crowds were thinning out, a little bandy rooster Italian guy in a solid goldish zoot suit and matching pork pie hat was giving our display AJ-2 bomber the big eye as he slowly walked completely around that aircraft while apparently analyzing it in some detail. After maybe 10 minutes or so, he sidled up to me as if expecting some inside information, identified himself as Tony in a very low, almost whisper, and quietly asked me questions about the AJ-2's top speed (I answered: *pretty darn fast for an aerial gas station*), maximum altitude, (*way up there above the clouds on a good day*), operational range (*quite a long ways, probably clear to Egypt from here*), maximum load capacity (*a big, heavy refueling tank full of fuel*), and specific stuff like that. Of course, I was trying to jolly him along without spilling the beans, especially the classified beans.

Then he commented on the large size of our closed bomb-bay doors and darn near demanded that I tell him what we really carried in there. Since I had been kidding the little guy as a diversion, I said "groceries" or something frivolous like that.

Obviously peeved at my answers, the little fellow proceeded to tell me in no uncertain terms (I can't remember his exact words after 63 years) that we carried a single Mark 15 atom bomb, those big reciprocating engines were R2800s, the jet in our tail assembly was a J-51 turbojet, our maximum altitude was 43,000 feet altitude and not the official 40,000 feet altitude, and with those fat laminar-flow wings, that AJ-2 would never hit 500 miles an hour except in a terminal dive, so they were mui vulnerable to the Soviet Mig-15.

The little guy was absolutely spot-on at every count. I tried to BS him as a diversion while I visually searched the crowded flight deck for Navy or Marine security guys. Finding none, I looked back to where the little guy had just been standing, but he had disappeared into the crowd. Although we were: (1) on a somewhat isolated ship three miles off shore; (2) all water transportation was controlled by the U.S. Navy; and (3) he could not have been more identifiable in that goldish zoot suit and matching pork pie hat if he had been a seven-foot tall, stacked, beautiful blond babe in a skimpy bikini; we never saw him again although we searched the Lake Champ from bow to stern and top to bottom. as well as every boatload of visitors that left our ship that day. That little guy must have been an Olympic class swimmer, or an awful good impersonator of an Italian nun.

By the way, I later heard similar stories from another VAH squadron in the Pacific Fleet. Although we weren't fooling anybody, friend or foe about the VAH squadrons' missions, the Navy never dropped the air-to-air refueling ruse while I was with VAH-7.

15. THE ROCK OF GIBRALTAR

We especially enjoyed the Rock of Gibraltar because we didn't have to play those fairly dicey wave-timing games to hop into or out of our liberty boats as they bobbed up and down with the waves. Those suckers are sometimes more than a dozen feet high from the wave trough to the wave crest while the aircraft carrier sat rock solid and immovable in the water like an island. If that won't get you puckered as you prepare to step onto or off of a small liberty boat, and the place where you were going to put your foot on your next step is suddenly a dozen feet or so above you or about the same distance below you, probably nothing will. Timing was everything, and after weeks of day and night flights, maintenance and repair operations, and intelligence scheming under incredibly exhausting conditions, very few said to heck with that and go back to the 24/7 "Big Floater" card game or whatever diversion they can find instead of going ashore on their hard-earned shore liberty.

However, at Gibraltar's handy dandy ship dock, all we had to do was salute the ship's Officer of the Deck, salute Old Glory on the quarterdeck, and step casually off the rock-solid ship and onto a rock-solid dock. I could have easily gotten used to that rare luxury very quickly.

The little town on Gibraltar is more like a small but lively village in England. They have all of the conveniences and necessities like pubs, grocery stores, haberdasheries, dry cleaning and alteration shops, curio vendors, etc., etc. However, unlike other Mediterranean villages, towns and cities, there were no houses of ill repute; at least none that we heard about. Actually, Gibraltar would have been absolutely idyllic if a bunch of our sailors hadn't rolled into a local pub, noticed a full size portrait of Her Majesty, the Queen of England, and one of those rascals asked the bartender who the heck was that bitch. I guess that some of those guys really did not know, or they thought that historically the large number of Scottish soldiers in that pub at that time would have little allegiance for the Queen of England.

Unfortunately, they were wrong. Si, Guy and I visited that pub maybe an hour later, and they were still wiping up the blood, sweeping away the broken glass, and hauling away the shattered furniture. However, as tradition dictated, they never stopped serving their ale by the pint.

That same afternoon, Si, Guy and I were lured into an ancient, essentially covered back alley by a large, beautiful, black pussy cat that seemed to be as tame as any lazy lap dog. I would have bet that cat weighed well over 20 pounds, so we figured that he/she must be a very talented rat-catching feline. Right away, we could see a lot of attractive possibilities if we could just sneak that cat aboard the USS Lake Champlain and into my always locked Squadron Air Intelligence Office. So the three of us pretty much cornered that cat and were in the process of five-finger adopting it when a door behind us opened to light up the whole alley, the shadow of a very large man fell over the three of us with room to spare, and a rumbling voice said something like: "Whatcha' doin' wit me cat?"

That British Sergeant Major must have been 6 feet and 10 inches tall, and looked like he was more than ready to defend his fat cat. So we switched gears and assured that big Limey that we were just admiring his fine big feline, and only wanted to see if his shiny black fur was as thick and smooth as it appeared to be. Somewhat mollified, the Sgt. Major invited us into a crowded army barracks and after introductions all around, he invited us to join in their Tea Time, which was just starting.

I swear, that was the best darned cup of tea that I have ever had, bar none. It seemed to be as thick as a cup of hot chocolate, had a rich hearty taste, and perfectly complemented the biscuits that came with the tea. No wonder their beer was room temperature and not worth a flip. An avid coffee drinker, I thought that I would never praise a cup of tea, but that tea was that good and I most certainly did.

That afternoon, we hitched a ride up to within climbing distance from the top of the Rock of Gibraltar. Then we climbed the rest of the way up to very top of that massive rock to take a look across the dozen or so miles at a haze that is Morocco.

A fairly large gaggle of wild Barbary Macaques monkeys—I looked the name up to flesh out this sea story—ran loose among the boulders at the top of the Rock of Gibraltar. These happy campers were independent and fairly tame as they begged for food from whoever showed up, as well as a couple of on-duty British zoologists who fed, cared for, and kept track of them. Apparently, each monkey was a distinct and identifiable individual, had an appropriately British name (like Herby and Chelsea), and a unique personality as well.

According to those zoologists, these animals were unique because several of them had been seen on both sides of the Straits of Gibraltar. Since they could not swim the turbulent straits that connect the Atlantic Ocean to the Mediterranean Sea, the zoologists said that they believed that an ancient tunnel lays under the strait that joins the two continents, and apparently no human has found either end.

How about those apples, Barbary Macaque monkey fans?

16. A FINE DAY IN PALERMO, SICILY

Hopelessly lost in the "King's Palace" in Palermo, Sicily—I had stopped to eyeball something really interesting and must have zigged where the palace guide and the rest of my tourist group zagged—so somehow I had wandered by accident into the residents' private living quarters. That was much like finding yourself in Bill and Hilary Clinton's livingroom during a messed-up White House tour.

Fortunately, I bumped into an attractive, obviously sophisticated young American gal who said she was also lost. Thank goodness, she spoke and read Italian fairly well, which helped us extract ourselves without further complications from what could have been a really messy international faux pas. I can just see the headline now: "Nosy American Dummy Captured In Bedroom Of King's Palace."

Since we shared that adventure and survived unscathed, we naturally bonded a bit, had a nice supper together in a fairly decent outdoor restaurant, toured the night lights of Palermo hand in hand so she would not trip and fall on the tricky cobblestone streets, shared a sack of rum-filled soft candy that almost blew my hat off, enjoyed adult beverages at a romantic street-side bistro, but never got all hot and bothered since she was the devoted if somewhat adventurous wife of the American Ambassador to somewhere; apparently neither Italy nor the Vatican. At least, that was what she told me, so like a wise man once said: "You just don't jump the bones of an American Ambassador's wife; at least not on the first cheap date."

As we parted late that night, I made the distinctly stupid mistake of offering her a tour the USS Lake Champlain if ever she had the time and inclination to stop by the ship. So darned if she didn't show up two weeks later while we were parked three miles off Naples, Italy—the atom bombs, you know—and had me paged from the ship's bridge, which was normally reserved for only the most important VIPs on high-level occasions. At least, someone up there fell for her story the way I probably should have.

Back in Ready Room One, a couple of our more politically oriented, social-climbing, older command pilots got all a'twitter about tagging along with me and meeting the American Ambassador's wife. Since I was in the middle of a grubby, greasy, overdue, high priority and highly classified air intelligence task anyway, I asked those senior pilots to take my place as her hosts aboard the ship. Then I escaped into VAH-7's Top Secret intelligence headquarters, locked the door, and finally finished that phase of my chores while not answering that door until well after all visitors were back on shore that evening.

Naturally, those two senior officers were all a'twitter. They figured that they were somewhat in debt to me, but I never bothered to bring it up again. After that, the squadron rumor mills had a field day about what might be my "real job" as well as that "PI" for "Political Influence" that was stamped on the upper right hand corner of the cover of my personnel file ever since I joined the squadron. You talk about whispered scuttlebutt galore. Once again, squadron rumors were so much better than the real thing, so I let the whole furschlugginger affair slide and didn't elaborate on anything to anybody.

As Mr. Cowboy, the night clerk at the Royal Hotel back in El Dorado, Kansas once said: "Never miss a good chance to shut up. It messes with gossipers' heads."

17. CLARE BOOTHE LUCE ALMOST VISITS US AT SEA.

On the subject of ambassadors, Clare Boothe Luce, our Ambassador to Italy, decided to visit the USS Lake Champlain while we were underway at sea. That was quite a big deal, and a heck of a lot of preparation went into that occasion. We not only had a "clean sweep-down fore and aft," but also a lot of painting, mopping and steam cleaning were mixed in that act as well. That was no surprise, but steaks for all of the ship's crew and the squadrons added up to something in excess of 3,500 steaks being cooked for one meal. That was something that even the old salts had never seen onboard an aircraft carrier before, and probably will never see again.

As the appointed hour arrived, the flight deck was cleared for Ambassador Luce's arrival in a WW II TBM torpedo bomber. Although the TBM looked like a pregnant, single-engine fighter plane from the late 1930s, that aircraft was the best choice for the mission. Tactically obsolete, the TBM was a very stable, dependable aircraft for aircraft carrier operations. It also delivered our mail several times each week while we cruised the clear blue Mediterranean Sea, so there was nothing new about it coming aboard while underway.

Unfortunately, The Powers That Be could not have picked a worse day for an arrested landing aboard the Lake Champ. Massive waves caused the fantail to rise and fall maybe 15 to 20 feet or more. That is indeed a booger bear. When landing, if the TBM got the "cut engine" order from our LSO when the fantail was just starting to fall, the TBM could fall an additional 20 feet in a full-stall landing. Not good! If the TBM was over the fantail and the LSO gave the "cut" order when the flight deck would be moving upward to collide with the TBM coming down, that could just about shove the pilot, crew's and VIP Ambassador's rear ends up between their shoulder blades. That's a figure of speech, but not far off the mark.

That TBM made seven or eight passes over our pitching flight deck above the foamy waves before someone called it off. Ambassador Luce could have called it off at any time that she pleased, but apparently she hung in there as her TBM made really hairy passes and wave-offs over and over again. Apparently, she was fearless and very determined, or else she was clueless. I would have aborted and gone back to the barn a whole lot earlier if I had been aboard that old war horse and had any say in the matter.

Since the steaks were already cooked, we all settled in for the best shipboard meal in many an old salt's memory. Along with the hot rolls, veggies, spuds, peach or apple cobbler desserts and unlimited coffee, we were good and plenty stuffed. As I got up to leave the lunch table, a cook I knew insisted that I eat another of his spare steaks. I had no choice in the matter and had to turn him down because I was stuffed to my giblets. But that cook offered more insistently, and I finally had to hot foot it out of that mess hall before he shoved it down my gullet.

As unbelievable as it may sound today, that was the historic moment in time when U.S. Navy cooks under way at sea could not even give away freshly cooked steaks.

18. OUR TOUR GUIDE WORE TWO HATS

One of the more persistent waterfront slicky boys in Naples was badgering the arriving sailors and Marines from the USS Lake Champlain to play house with his sister or some other female relative. Incredibly persistent, he scurried along hawking their wares on the edge of a group of U.S. servicemen who wanted nothing to do with that sleazy rascal or any woman who would have anything to do with a skuzz bag like him.

Finally, Si and I got really tired of his pestering and ducked into a grand old cathedral near the bay. We thought that we would lose that nasty rascal that way. Besides that, as a one-time architectural student in college, Si was interested in the medieval architecture and some of the massive restoration projects underway after being heavily bombed by us during WW II.

Surprisingly, that rascal followed us inside the cathedral, switched to his tour guide mode, and conducted a fairly decent tour of the whole edifice, its history, and a play-by-play account of the ongoing repairs to the WW II bomb damage. We were thoroughly impressed by the depth of his knowledge and the time that he put in that very interesting project, so he collected a well-earned fee from us for his excellent presentation. However, as soon as we stepped back outside the cathedral, that greasy little son of a sea cook began badgering us again to play house at a newly reduced special price with his sister, his beautiful cousin or whoever; each of whom was, of course, as pure as the driven snow.

Tell me another one, Tony. I too was born at night, but that was not last night.

19. AWOL ALL DAY IN SUNNY BARCELONA, SPAIN

Tired of carrying other guys' water too often, Si and I went AWOL (i.e., absent without official leave) in Barcelona, Spain, after our Commanding Officer postponed liberty call until the three plane captains, with every enlisted man in the detachment's assistance, wiped down every inch of all three AJ-2 bombers with gasoline to quickly clean them, and then rub oil on them to protect the painted sheet metal from the salty environment.

Long story short; that definitely was not our job. In fact, each plane captain received extra flight skins (i.e., extra pay) for doing that and other jobs on his assigned bomber. So Si and I eased over and stood liberty inspection with another squadron whose C.O. didn't know that he didn't know us. Then, we went ashore the first thing in the morning while the rest of our VAH-7 mates changed from their Class "A" liberty uniforms into dungarees and essentially did a large chunk of those three plane captains' jobs for them. I really liked each of those plane captains, but none of them gave me a hand when I worked 16 hours a day or even more at my several jobs. Enough said.

At the first kiosk ashore, which was the first watering hole on the waterfront boulevard, we each had a couple of cognacs for openers, and then went to my first bull fight where 50,000 or more rabid Spanish aficionados yelled "Olay!" for the toreador (i.e., bull fighter) whenever he did something laudable in the ring with the bull. However, Si and I were the only ones in that huge stadium yelling "Olay!" when the bulls had their way. Fortunately, the Spanish crowd was unconditionally tolerant of just two snockered gringos in uniform.

After about an hour of exciting entertainment, Generalissimo Franco quietly entered his personal box through a hidden hatch with no fanfare whatsoever. As each Spaniard in the crowd noticed Franco's unannounced entry, he or she quietly stood up and faced Franco to show their respect. Finally, everyone in the entire stadium including Si and I were standing quietly facing Franco except for the toreador, who still had his hands full with irritating the heck out of that raging, pissed-off bull.

When the toreador finally noticed what was happening, he too stopped, turned around and stood at attention facing Franco as the bull ran over him and gored him fairly badly. Si and I held our "Olay!" for another day. We weren't that snockered.

The morale: some bulls cannot be trusted when it comes to politics. The same might be said for elephants and jackasses, left and right, in American politics back in the states.

20. NAVY STYLE DISCIPLINE

After splitting up earlier that evening, Si finally found me well after midnight in a small but raucous waterfront bar on a narrow side alley near the bay. I was having a blast as three generations of gypsies introduced me to an exhausting tarantella on a small but crowded dance floor while I was introducing them to the Arapahoe war cry. Despite the late hour, Si and I were not allowed to leave the bar until every male gypsy in the building shook our hands, and several of the matriarchs gave us hugs and their blessings. Funny thing, I have never again been able to do that gypsy tarantella dance again even though I was sure that I was doing it so darned well that night.

Since all U.S. sailors and Marines had long since returned to their ships, we were in a heap of trouble until Si pulled some strings with a Navy helmsman who owed Si a favor, so that we could ride the three miles over water back to the Lake Champ with the Fleet Admiral in his private motor launch. When you talk about a taciturn admiral that night, you have to mention that one although he would make it up to me later on. Heck, I washed my hands in seawater before I saluted him, but I guess that he wanted to be alone with his private thoughts that night.

The next morning as I was plotting the mission coordinates and briefing data for that night's flight operations, our detachment C.O. confronted me in the Ready Room about Si and I going on liberty without permission while all of the rest of the enlisted guys were hard at work doing the jobs for which the plane captains got their flight pay for not flying very much. Really torqued, the C.O. concluded his tight-jawed tirade with the pointed threat that he could toss Si and I into the brig for our faux pas if he wanted to.

I thought about that for a couple of nanoseconds, then closed my pre-mission folder, pushed it across the table toward him, and told him with all due respect that I was really exhausted after that long night and early revile. And since I was such good friends with all of the Marines down at the brig, I would probably enjoy a couple of days of R&R in those very comfortable accommodations.

At that, the C.O. leaned across my conference table, spanked the back of my hand twice with his open hand, and said: "Don't ever do that again." Then he left the ready room walking kind of tight assed like he had an egg jammed up his fanny and his dignity all tattered and torn. I had to bite the inside of my cheek to keep from busting out laughing before the door closed.

Say what! Air wing discipline was a heck of a lot different than that for mud Marines. I would have loved a couple of days of R&R tucked in the comforts of that Marine brig, but our C.O. had no backups for either Si or I, so he was stuck with us and he darned well knew it.

21. NAVY/MARINE "E" FOR EXCELLENCE AWARD

VAH-7 won the Navy/Marine "E" for Excellence while operating on the USS Lake Champlain, CVA 39 in the summer of 1955. Nobody was more surprised than the guys in our detachment. That was such an irony; such a mind-boggling, inconceivable thought considering all of the negative ear banging that we had endured from so many different directions. Think about it; since VAH-7 had won the big "E" and received that unit commendation and the ribbon to display on our liberty uniforms, what in the world could be the condition of the other heavy attack squadrons that did not win? I could only guess, and the thought was a little scary.

However, after taking all of that heat from on high, my under-the-table reports to "the Boss" spelled out chapter and verse about how our detachment maintenance guys working in the hanger deck and on the flight deck had improved our combat readiness despite the mind-boggling requirements for 12-man-hours of maintenance for every hour that each of the three AJ bombers were in the air, as well as working around the clock day after day with up to 60-knot (68 mph) winds blowing across the flight deck—30-knot winds and stronger with the ship steaming at 30 knots into that wind to launch or land our lumbering "whales" during flight operations—both day and night in good weather and bloody awful storms.

I backed up those data with proprietary mission data blended with timed maintenance logs and personal as well as combined flight-log data that no one else could compile. And despite their generally negative layers of elitist, fraternity guy attitudes, our C.O., X.O. and the rest of the pilots and bombardier/navigators had overcome all obstacles to accomplish almost all of our mission objectives. I was assigned to VAH-7 to indirectly tell the Navy Department what was happening and why, and that is what they got; game, set, and match.

Three weeks later, after we transferred to the USS Coral Sea, CVA-43, our squadron C.O.—we called him Captain Elmer Fudd because he looked a bit like bald headed Elmer Fudd the cartoon character—flew in from his two miles long land-based runway at Port Lyautey, French Morocco, to the Naples land-based runways, then took the Coral Sea's launch to the ship and walked aboard the carrier while it was anchored three miles offshore. Although everyone in our detachment already knew all about our award for three whole weeks, ol' Elmer called a morning formation of all hands on the flight deck in "Class A" uniforms and grandly announced that yes indeed, VAH-7 had won the Navy/Marine E and that—this is verbatim—"I want you men to know that I could not have done this without you." Say what! Those were his exact words, and every guy in our detachment was blown away by them.

Afterward, as we switched back to our dungarees and went back to our daily chores, not one man in our squadron detachment acted as if he had even heard what our self-congratulatory Commanding Officer said. Even our detachment officers seemed to be embarrassed. Would you believe that about a year after returning to the United States, "Captain Elmer Fudd" was promoted to "Admiral Elmer Fudd?" Who'da thunk it? He probably did a bunch of good things that we did not know about; things way above our pay grades.

Talk about being short shifted, I had to go begging to Marine squadron VMF 222 to borrow a doggoned paint spray gun to paint the Navy E on all three of our bombers. And then, despite the fact that it was not in my job description nor any way expected, I cut 18-inch stencils and borrowed masking tape to personally paint the Navy E on each AJ bomber because, get this, we did not have a single maintenance guy able or qualified to paint that simple design on our aircraft in our whole darned furschlugginger 100-man maintenance and repair detachment.

By then, I was having so much fun painting again—I spray painted airplanes at Beechcraft all one summer on the graveyard shift when I was in junior college—that I painted most of the helmets for our flight crews and plane captains, and did a passably decent job personalizing each of those helmets—eagles wings, Nordic animal horns, and even big bloodshot eyeballs—before I returned all of the painting equipment to the Marine squadron. But I did not get the big head because I never did figure out how VMS 222 painted those perfect black and white checkerboards on their curved fuselages and round helmets.

However, I didn't lose any sleep over that deficiency. My whole focus at that time was to "get 'er done." We were, indeed, a "can do" operation even though many of our maintenance requirements were impossible to accomplish with our available resources. It seemed as if the wheels were coming off our little red wagon and nobody wanted to fall on his sword to sort out our many problems.

23. LAMBORGHINI TAXI CAB'S RACE

After a gala and much-deserved Detachment 31 party in a roadhouse high in the rugged mountains west of Palermo, Sicily, I woke up in the head (i.e., the potty) hugging the porcelain convenience and listening to the dead silence. Everyone else and the hired buses had left to return to the ship long before my rude awakening. So I washed my face, took a whizz, wandered out to the nearby highway, and stuck out my thumb. Almost immediately, a tall, slim Italian playboy driving an extremely expensive, low and powerful Lamborghini sports/racing car stopped and picked me up. By my watch, I had about 10 minutes before the last liberty boat would depart for the ship at midnight, and we were at about 15 miles of winding mountain roads away.

However, we made it just under the wire in a spectacular four-wheel drift off the road and onto the dock proper. I guess that when you own a Lamborghini, every conversation seems like another driving challenge.

But try to visualize just how fast that low-slung race car had to be traveling on steep mountain switchbacks with only its parking lights on and its driving lights turned off at night except for a momentary flash as we entered each new curve. Thank God for a full moon. Only the ship's cleaners knew just how tense I was.

Then, imagine the flurry on the dock when the lost sheep (yours truly) finally showed up in a $200,000 luxury racing car back when $200,000 was a heck of a lot of money. When I literally crawled out of that low-slung car to make a dash to the last liberty boat of that night, my Italian chauffeur impulsively jumped out of his side of the car, scurried around the front bumper and hugged me like a long-lost brother or a very dear old friend. Then he literally jumped back into his race car and took off at darned near, heck, I don't know how fast it was, but it was darned fast by the time that he blew through the dock area and hit the highway in a tire-squealing four-wheel drift. Over in less than a minute, the whole show was just flat spectacular.

Just for the halibut, I was careful to never tell any of our guys what really happened that night. More grist for the rumor mill, I was quietly enjoying feeding them juicy slices to supplement the scuttlebutt already being passed around. That certainly helped to make the time go by. Our squadron's imagination was much better than the real thing, and once again, my silence spoke volumes untold.

Mea maxima culpa, or as Roger Miller liked to sing: "Dang me. Dang me. They oughta' take a rope and hang me. High from the highest tree; woman would you weep for me, bap, bap, bap; woman would you weep for me?"

23. CHEAP EXTRACURRICULAR FIRE INSURANCE

While approaching a hatch from the ship's superstructure to the flight deck, a loud explosion was followed by the boson's whistle over the intercom, a series of terse commands, and the pounding of many feet headed in my direction. As I stepped aside and held the hatch open for a stack of sailors running toward the aft end of the flight deck, I saw smoke and fire from what was left of an F9F fighter airplane scattered all over the aft flight deck. Every sailor was running to their emergency stations; everyone but the flight deck fire fighter in the bright silver rig with enclosed head, feet, hands, and full body protective gear.

That rig was entirely too heavy for actual running, but this incredible guy walked rapidly into the raging fire with no hesitation, disappearing into that inferno as streams of water and fire retardant made very little apparent headway against the sea of burning JP-4 aviation fuel.

Seemingly only a few moments later, the guy in the silver suit reappeared carrying the unconscious pilot wrapped in a silver fireproof blanket that matched the flight deck fire fighter's protective gear. As soon as they cleared the actual flames but were still in a place that was too hot for most people, the flight deck personnel and corpsmen rushed forward to put the injured pilot on a stretcher and quickly hustled him to the ship's medical facilities.

The possibility of a second explosion within the wreckage seemed to make no difference. Each sailor had a particular job to do, and he did it without hesitation just like he was trained to do; over and over again. You would have been proud of every single one of them. I certainly was.

That whole operation made me think. What if I would be in another crash with a raging fire like that? What if there was another guy or two in that fire with me? Of course, I want the guy in the silver fire suit to recognize his good friend, Dave, and get me the heck out of there mui pronto. All I needed was an introduction and some trade goods to seal the deal.

The next afternoon, I found the guy in the silver fire suit sitting quietly behind the ship's superstructure as he watched the deck apes preparing for incoming aircraft. I was carrying two ice-cold cokes and supposedly looking for Big Swig. I'll call the guy in the silver suit, Frank—because I don't remember his name—had not seen Swig all day, probably because Swig was sleeping off a late night flight and I knew it. So I gave Frank the cold coke rather than let it go to waste.

Naturally, we talked a while before the recovery operations began, and we discovered that each of us had a Mexican blood brother. His was another E'se bueno hombre from the hood; mine was permanent Pfc. Eladio Gonzales from the 5th Marines. Not only that, but we both preferred brown-eyed girls with long hair and lacy mantillas for Sunday Mass. Blue-eyed brunettes were ok too. There's a handy coincidence for consideration.

I wrote Dad, and he sent me the latest Playboy Magazine that I requested. It was not available in the Mediterranean Theatre at that time. Dad wrote: "What do you want that for?" I wrote back: "Don't worry Dad, that's trade goods." Dad understood.

Apparently, Frank had not seen Playboy before, or at least not that issue. When it arrived, I gave it to Frank, centerfold and all. Then, when we dropped anchor at Palma, Majorca, Frank had not had time to visit the ship's barber, so he was rejected as he tried to get on the liberty boat. I saw the problem, got off the liberty boat with Frank, borrowed a hair clipper and gave him a quick crew cut. Both of us got on a following liberty boat with no problems at all.

Bottom line: I believed that I had extracurricular fire insurance for on-deck emergencies, and a pretty good friend in the deal. How's that for a two-fer?

24. PROMOTION BY DEFAULT

On our second or third visit to Majorca, I was back at my favorite table at my favorite outdoor bar drinking my favorite rum and Cocoa Cola beverage high up on the steepest hill in downtown Palma. Suddenly, I heard the erratic roar of a fast-revving motor cycle engine just below me, followed by a loud series of individual crashes and the sounds of metal scraping and glass breaking, and then somebody who was hurting a heck of a lot.

Somehow I just knew that meant trouble for us, so I slugged down the last of my sipping beverage and ran down the steep hill past the Brit fern bar and around the corner where I found our squadron's Air Intelligence Officer, my boss, laying in the street next to a wiped-out British murder cycle. Even at first glance, I could see that his leg was obviously broken.

Everyone in the black-shoe Sixth Fleet and the various squadron detachments had direct orders to never even think about driving murder cycles while on liberty. Therefore, in addition to his broken leg, my boss was in deep doo doo and in danger of at least a Captain's Mast or worse as soon as he could hobble around with the aid of crutches. That was not good.

So I asked a couple of passing Marine friends to drag the murder cycle around the corner out of sight while I rented a riding horse with saddle for $20 from a nearby stable while another Marine and a kindly streetwalker made Ed comfortable until I returned with the horse. When the Shore Patrol (SP) and Navy corpsmen finally arrived, the cause of Ed's injuries was obvious: he had fallen off a cantankerous but street legal riding horse, which was sad, but certainly not a court-marshal offense.

Hell's bells; we all lie a little.

I never saw Ed again, even after we returned to our new home base at Sanford, Florida, so I was stuck with the $20 rent for the horse. If you are reading this, Ed; with interest you owe me a metric pot-full of ready whipout. I will take cash, personal checks, cashier's checks or anything else that can be converted for me to buy the frivolous stuff that I often purchase.

Later, after the Coral Sea got underway, I heard that Ed was taken by an emergency flight off the carrier to Port Lyautey, and then back to the United States. No one on crutches has any business being on an aircraft carrier at sea.

Here is the crazy part: Ed was not replaced, not even by a junior officer. To everyone's amazement, mine the most of all, I was assigned by default to take over Ed's job as Squadron Air Intelligence guru on an "interim basis." Not only that, but Ed was never replaced while we were overseas.

Air intelligence/mission briefings/planning and coordination for our VAH-7 atomic bombers at the point of the NATO/US spear never missed a beat. We just kept on keeping on. After that, I don't think that I fooled too many in the squadron about my actual assignment, but we continued with the subterfuge just the same, and my life got a bit more complicated as most of the enlisted men toned down or stopped bad mouthing VAH-7 in my presence.

As T. S. Eliot once said: "Human kind cannot bear very much reality."

25. ATHENS' ACROPOLIS AFTER DARK

There we were on liberty at the historic Acropolis of Athens, Greece. I had seen it so many times in movies and magazines, read about it in half a dozen history books and historic novels, and then, by golly, I was actually there (figure 15). The whole place was amazing and awe inspiring. I was almost giddy that I was there and enjoying every minute of it. So my good buddy, Guy Garafalo and I made the most of it. Guy called himself "Ginny," and since I came from southern Kansas, I thought that was his real name until Si gave me the word about Guy's nickname.

Figure 15. Acropolis of Athens-Original Porch of the Maidens

Guy and I walked around the entire ruins for hours taking color slides while building many wonderful memories. As evening approached, I decided that I had to get some pictures of a colorful sunset over the mountains to the west as seen through the ancient columns of this very special place. Wow, what a memento that was. So I setup up my camera and took a bunch of slides until darkness settled over us and cancelled my photo session.

As Guy and I were preparing to leave, we noticed a sudden influx of apparently local civilians, mostly couples, walking two by two up the steep marble stairs to the main ruins. Then we saw some of those couples lying down in the rubble as the dark shadows obstructed most normal details. But then, lo and behold, it seemed that the sound levels of the activities around us were increasing exponentially while accompanied by quite a bit of scuffling, giggling and rustling around. What in the heck was going on? I should have known right away, but I just couldn't get my mind wrapped around the truth until there was no denying the obvious.

For crying out loud, after dark the ancient, world-famous Athenian Acropolis become an open-air house of, no, make that a temple of ill repute, or was that some kind of ancient fertility rite? That question was soon answered by the madam who appeared at the bottom of those storied marble steps as we walked down. Right away, she tried to rent us some half-naked gal masked in shadows and just a few veils with whom to make whoopee on a bed of ancient marble rubble. All we knew about her was that she too was "as pure as the mountain snows."

Like they say: "Different strokes for different folks. That little gal was so darned short she could have modeled for trophies," so we tipped our hats and passed right on down those famous marble stairs.

26. WITH FRIENDS LIKE THESE, WHO NEEDS ENEMIES?

The next day, Si and I were playing silly games as we crossed an immense, barbed-wire-enclosed, barren field just west of the ancient Acropolis at Athens. Full of Uzo and hippity hopping from boulder to boulder to ancient temple rubble, etc. to settle a mutual bet, neither of us put a foot down on the rocky soil for well over 150 yards or so from the south section of fence nearest the Acropolis to the north section of fence by the ruins of the ancient Grecian market place.

Later, back aboard the ship, we discovered a pre-liberty warning pamphlet to all hands that stated that field was an uncleared and very dangerous mine field left over from the Greek Civil War in 1949. The warning signs on the fence were written in Greek with no international warning or recognizable emblems for us unsuspecting nonGreeks.

Si and I had wondered why those two Greek teenagers gave us directions on how to cut across that fenced area, but then they romped around the outside of that large field while never taking their eyes off our progress as we jumped from boulder to rubble to boulder just for the pure fun of it. We seemed to be the featured entertainment for those kids, although we did not know it at that time. I guess we should have taken a bow after we completed crossing that essentially unmarked but still lethal mine field, but we were too busy sharing our last bottle of Uzo and taking bou coup color slides.

Like they say, you can never tell what Greek teenagers might do after they become bored with the ancient architectural antiquities. With friends like those, who the heck needs enemies?

27. READY ROOM "TALKER" BY DEFAULT

Just after lunch, we had a terribly messy jet aircraft crash and raging fire that slid to a stop on the flight deck directly above VAH-7's Ready Room One. The fire and several really loud explosions were on the other side of our heavy steel ceiling structure, and burning jet fuel began dripping down through some of the damage on the teak wood deck overlying our steel flight deck and into the middle of our ready room. The ship's fire and crash crews were all over the fire on the flight deck, but they were still not winning the battle when I was volunteered by default—I was the only guy still in our Ready Room because I was hurriedly picking up highly classified documents, so naturally I got the rose after all of the pilots and crews bugged out—to be the Ready Room "Talker" on the intra-ship intercom because the regular Ready Room Talker was in the head (i.e., bathroom) and then cut off from his usual duty station by the hellacious fire in the cross-deck passageway as well as the flight deck inferno.

As the raging, roaring inferno directly overhead cooked the Ready Room hotter and hotter, and drops of burning aviation fuel were dripping even more than before from the overhead structure onto the ready room deck (i.e., floor) and furniture nearby in much bigger blobs, I called the Primary Flight (Pri-Fly) Operations officer, curtly reported the self-barbecue situation at Ready Room One, and asked why the heck the newly anointed Ready Room Talker (yours truly) had to stay at this post under such iffy conditions.

Pri-Fly's answer: "Hold your post. Pri-Fly must maintain direct contact with all ready rooms," as if we were conducting normal business as usual. However, after seeing more and bigger burning globs steadily falling for a couple of minutes plus or minus several heartbeat hiccups, my response was something like: "Not good enough, Sir! Ready Room One, out." Pri-Fly responded: "Say again, Ready Room One." Me: "Sayonara Sir. I'm getting the heck outa' Dodge while I'm still alive."

Our Ready Room was fairly well scorched, and a lot of fire and smoke-damaged furniture and equipment needed rapid replacement. I figured that I had done the right thing because I was not replaceable as far as I was concerned. Granted, maybe I wasn't much on the grand scale of all things nautical, but I was all of the "me" that I had, and that was enough reason to boogy on out the door with or without Pri-Fly's impersonal permission.

28. FARMER DAVE (SAY WHAT?)

The bus ride from Naples to Rome to see Pope Pius XII and drink red wine in quantities untold took a lot longer than we expected. Big Swig came off the farm to join the Navy in 1936, and he had just recently made a down payment on his retirement farm in Pennsylvania. He, his wife and their children planned to retire there in mid1956. Swig did not fool around. He knew the soil acidity of every corner of his new farm, and we spent the major part of that long bus ride with Swig discussing the chemicals and preparatory crops that would improve the land to the proper balance to grow the various crops that he wanted.

Actually, Swig talked about all of that scientific A&M Aggie stuff, and I just sat there looking out the bus window while enjoying the Italian scenery. I did nod once in a while when it seemed appropriate, but mostly to show Swig that I was still awake.

Although I was raised in Kansas where a lot of wheat is harvested and the tall corn grows—but not as well as in Iowa—I grew up in the low-rent part of Wichita and certainly not on a farm. What little I knew about farming came from rooming for a little more than a semester with the Girrens twins, Mike and Lou, whose daddy owned a large farm just southwest of Wichita—which is now called Wichita International Airport—hunting and camping on Kansas farm land, working on my cousins' truck farm, and listening to my Grampa George Volz ramble on and on about his huge corn, cattle and hog farm north of Des Moines, Iowa.

Bottom line, I had heard little bits and pieces about various farm stuff hither and yon, and I would continue to listen intently to Grampa's stories as long as he kept bringing those locker boxes full of his fan-danged-tastic smoked sausage every time that he and Grandma Amy visited my family in Wichita. But overall, I really did not know boo doodly about the best ways to manage a successful dirt farm, and I never once implied that I did.

However, Swig was so darn intense about farming in general, and so enthusiastic about his new farm that an occasional nod or "Yeah, that sounds okay" muttered answer must have seemed to validate his plans when he was talking about crop rotation, farm equipment and prepping the soil for too much or too little acidity.

Actually, about all that Swig knew about my background was that I came from Kansas on the Great Plains, and I was a good listener if it didn't interrupt my sight-seeing. However, when we got back to the ship, Swig told Si and Guy "that Dave Ferman is the best damned farmer I've ever known." Say what? Sometimes it pays to just shut up, nod every so often, and keep smiling. Farmer Dave, aye? Nebba' hotchee, yankee gringo sod buster.

29. ROME HAS MANY ATTRACTIONS.

During my six days of touring in Rome, I was blown away by the Vatican where we were welcomed by Pope Pius XII, toured all of the major churches in the city—each one more ornate than the previous church—as well as the coliseum, the pantheon, etc., etc., dozens of really big, ornate fountains, and more darned bars and night clubs in the evenings than I could remember even if I had stayed sober. A ten-cent pack of Lucky Strike cigarettes would open almost any door in Rome, so we all carried a pack in our shirt pockets, and one or two packs at the ankle in each stocking for quick access, and a full carton in my luggage wnen traveling cross country. Hershey bars were also pure gold, so I always had one or two tucked away when leaving the ship on liberty, and a box full for Rome.

As luck would have it, I had a very nice room by myself in a decent hotel on Via Della Conciliazione, which was only a couple of blocks down the main street to the main entrance of the Vatican where we had that group audience with Pope Pius XII, and were blown away with all of the incredible artwork on such a grand scale from ceiling to floor. On the third or fourth day there, I was taking a short afternoon break from all of the mind boggling church decorations and Roman ruins in such abundance that they tumbled my gimbals. When I pulled back the shade and looked out the one window in my room, I unexpectedly enjoyed an inspirational view of St. Peter's Basilica while looking across the sleek, tanned backside of a lovely Italian ciao bella who was sunbathing on the flat roof of a hotel one floor below me. She was au naturale except for the tiny wisp of an almost invisible skin-colored bikini bottom, "and her hair hung down in ringlets; cha, cha, cha."

The total impression, the juxtaposition of youthful lust and the Seat of Church Moral Authority and Majesty, was an incredible dichotomy for a young and somewhat impressionable "fish-eating" lad from far off Kansas. But that did not stop me from looking out that window several more times just to make sure that young lady was still there and safe in all of her suntanned, exhibitionist glory. I'll bet that my battered Guardian Angel, Holy Joe, and Beelzebub himself must have had a battle royal for my soiled soul that soft and sunny afternoon. Holy Joe must have won that battle because I did not do what I think I could probably have done.

30. KEEN COMPETITION—THE LOSERS WON

We had two squadrons of FJ Fury fighter planes—USAF F86Ds redesigned for USN/USMC operations; i.e., beefed up fuselages to accommodate the rigors of aircraft carrier tail-hook landings, heavier shock absorbers and shorter wings for full-stall landings, marinized to offset the very salty/rust-prone environment of the oceans, etc.—onboard the USS Coral Sea and the USS Ticonderoga aircraft carriers. However, between both aircraft carriers, the black shoe Navy only had space for just one FJ-Fury (figure 16) squadron at a time.

Figure 16. FJ-Fury Fighter Aircraft

The Marine squadron, VMF 222, was scheduled to go back home because their tour was pretty much completed. The Navy squadron was scheduled to stay aboard the two ships until after Christmas. However, the Soviets had intensified their saber rattling and threatened mutual destruction galore if the U.S. Navy did not wise up, give up, and go home post haste. That's when some high-ranking ring-knocking flag officer in the War Department decided that the 6th Fleet needed the overall best FJ Fury fighter squadron at that time to protect all of our ships from the Soviet Air Force.

Therefore, the Navy and Marine FJ squadrons were pitted against each other in an intense, all-day, head-to-head competition to see which squadron was the most combat-ready. The winner would stay in the sunny Mediterranean; the loser would go home for retraining and home cooking.

Long story short, the Marines won that competition hands down for readiness, turnaround times, aerial and strafing gunnery, interceptions and whatever else indicated which squadron was more combat ready. You name it, the Marines won it impressively. However (surprise, surprise), that turned out to be bad news for the Marines and their families because they were forthwith extended something like six months in the Mediterranean Theater, and the Navy squadron happily turned around, folded their newly unfolded tents, and went back home after only a very short time on station at the point of the American spear.

Since the Navy FJ squadron had been a pretty darned good squadron up until that competition, some of our guys in the peanut gallery had good reason to be suspicious that the Navy squadron deliberately blew the competition so that they could go home early. On the other hand, the Marine squadron, being Marines (you know how we are), did not want to lose anything to a Navy squadron, so they gave their all, their very best, even though they fully understood the consequences. That's Marines in a nutshell. Semper fi, and forget Christmas at home.

As a casual observer, I had wondered why the Marine pilots and ground crews scrambled to their aircraft on the run while the Navy pilots walked out to their aircraft and took what seemed like an extra-long time kicking tires, lighting the fires, strapping in and launching. Could it be that a soon-to-retire Navy squadron commander decided to give his guys an early Christmas present?

Like they say: "Never trust a sailor who is quietly smiling at you but won't tell you why he is so contented. That will mess with your head."

31. BEIRUT — "THE PARIS OF THE MEDITERRANEAN"

The night before the USS Coral Sea dropped several anchors three miles off-shore at Beirut, Lebanon, I received a heads-up from my never-identified contact who I euphemistically called "the Boss." Something unexpected and apparently quite serious had happened in Beirut and the top brass on station urgently needed a lot more intelligence people to temporarily backfill that shortage until more qualified intelligence specialists could be relocated and assembled. Although my Military Occupational Specialty (MOS) did not particularly match that particular situational description, someone in the Boss's staff must have thought that I could contribute in some way.

Actually, I only qualified by default. Ever since my fearless leader, Lieutenant Ed, broke his leg riding a motorcycle—a punishable "No No" for all military personnel in the Sixth Fleet—and was flown back to the United States for extensive recovery, I remained the only acting Air Intelligence Specialist with VAH-7. If WW III would suddenly break out, VAH-7 could be the first to attack Mother Russia and I would be the guy who would coordinate that operation and then be the fourth crewman on the third and last atom bomber to launch from the USS Coral Sea.

At that time, I still did not know that Lieutenant Ed would not be replaced for some inconceivable reason, or that I would be thoroughly swamped with both his command job and my many subordinate tasks until after VAH-7 returned to the United States in late December of 1955. To me, that inconceivable situation had to be either an incredible screw-up beyond the realm of reason, or there was an Air Intelligence officer named Dave Ferman somewhere in the U.S. Navy, and we would all have a big laugh about that SNAFU (i.e., "situation normal: all fouled up") somewhere downstream.

Never-the-less, I had my orders to report to the senior Navy spook in Beirut eee-mediately if not sooner. Until further notice, I had to get with the program and do whatever that assignment required until that upper management faux pas would be sorted out and I could go back to being a comfortable second banana.

Actually, in addition to my original assignment to report on the combat readiness of VAH-7 to "the Boss" on the sly, I was kind of, sort of, maybe qualified for this unexpected extension of my job description. After all, I was formerly a mud Marine rifleman with leadership experience as a working Marine Drill Instructor (DI), a Military Policeman (MP), a Marine Guard at the Top-Secret Ames Laboratory near San Francisco, and the Cadet Battalion Commander at the Pensacola Flight Training Command for about a year. But possibly the most relevant qualification of all, I was handy and could hit the ground running as soon as the USS Coral Sea arrived at Beirut early the next morning.

Since intelligence specialists were coming to Beirut from Europe and the Mediterranean for the immediate emergency, the first order of business was to assemble all of the intelligence specialists assigned to this project so we could recognize each other while working undercover in the same general area. Therefore, about a dozen of us gathered in a back-alley storage/conference room at one of the elegant Paris-based stores that fronted on the famous divided boulevard that bordered the gorgeous Mediterranean waterfront.

However, as soon as we were assembled, I had an eerie, stomach-churning feeling about these certifiably professional spooks. Most of them wore too similar lightweight tropical suits so that they looked a bit like peas in a pod when assembled in one place.

But worse yet, after the get-acquainted, come-to-Jesus séance was over, as we were departing en-masse to go our separate ways to jumpstart the initial phases of that mission—rather than walk away quietly one or two at a time in various directions—several of those former Ivy League fraternity flakes actually saluted their superior officers as they parted. Those stupid damned thoughtless screw-ups occurred in the same alley where several small groups of those "insignificant rag heads" were idly hanging around in the shade chewing their khat stimulant and apparently doing very little else except watching everything that moved or breathed. Surely, that motley mob of Arab homeboys in their raggedy clothes would not notice anything like our guys' careless mental blunders.. Oh hell no. Heaven forbid.

The fact that those "funny" little Muslim guys with their knee-high crotches in their baggy, saggy trousers that fit tight around their ankles, and well-worn head wraps had been honing their spying skills for centuries and probably could have given our professional spooks an advanced course in sleuthing. Apparently, that never troubled some of our guys' happy thoughts. I hate to say it, but some of our gentlemen intelligence spooks seemed more like sophomoric fraternity pukes from elitist Ivy League colleges like Harvard, Yale, Princeton, etc., who were getting pumped up to go to a panty raid at some darn sorority house.

Give me a break. That operation was not a game. People could get hurt, permanently, and I sure as heck did not want to be one of the casualties because of a few elite underachievers.

By the way, when I asked about those local home-boys' choice of garb, I was told that the Mahdi, the long-anticipated Muslim Messiah, would be born of a man rather than of a woman. Therefore, the baggy trousers were intended to accommodate that holy baby's birth, and the tight fit at the ankles was intended to keep that baby from falling to the ground during the birthing process. The anticipated "final teacher" before the foretold "end of days," those Muslim men believed that the Imam Mahdi, together with the second coming of Jesus Christ, will defeat the false Messiah that is the Antichrist.

The bottom line, if our guys had any sense at all, they would keep their big mouths shut in public with respect to Muslim men's clothes. But that's exactly what a blabber-mouthed Navy intelligence desk jockey did not do; probably as some sort of twisted joke. Hell's bells, half of the Muslim guys in that narrow alley had to hear that clown. As I walked away, I could feel a large, itchy target forming on my back between my shoulder blades.

Anyway, despite everything to the contrary, there I was in suburban east Beirut trying to look like an innocuous Canadian tourist among individually hospitable—but often quite hostile when in groups—Muslims, Jews and even Christians when they were PO'ed. Meanwhile, several of our spooks who had been cannon cockers in another life, began unpacking and assembling their equipment to plot artillery target and fire-base coordinates around the geologic bowl in which the Beirut airport is located.

Several of our spooks, including yours truly, backed up the former "red legs" wherever and however we were needed both inside and outside the airport perimeters. If the "fit would ever hit the shan," or however that old saying goes, as a Marine, they depended on me to rush to the source of the trouble and make a difference. Maybe my past life as a 17-year-old bouncer in a hell-raising Kansas roadhouse in the oil patch trumped everything else in my record of accomplishments.

As you may have guessed by now, the urgent angst that generated this hurry-up-and-wait operation did not fully fester until 1957. At least, we were not playing catchup like we usually did in that region. So what the heck jumpstarted all of that sudden scrambling around and bouncing off the bulkheads? None among us knew for sure, but a recently strong undercurrent of anti-American, anti-Christian, anti-western sentiments was brewing in a number of local and suburban neighborhoods. Unresolved, that situation could lead to almost anything, including military intervention.

According to the latest master plan, several of the intel guys from our group would soon be sent to the Holy Lands to find the best tactical helicopter landing zones (LZs) for interlocking artillery fire bases on the east side of the Jordan River. Primarily, these guys would covertly checkout half a dozen pre-plotted LZs from the ground that had previously been identified as possible sites by high-altitude U2 aircraft. If none were up to snuff, our guys would then search the desert to find more tactically acceptable LZs/artillery fire bases from which a U.S. Marine blocking force could engage Israel's less-than-friendly neighbors if they decided to revert to the pre-1947 borders when there was no Israel.

Just for giggles, I raised my hand to volunteer for that mission. Fat chance of that, but what the heck. I figured that this unscheduled operation in Beirut would continue at least as long as the Coral Sea would be anchored three miles off Beirut, so I needed to cancel my prepaid tour of Jerusalem and that general area. With our foreseeable workload, I knew that I would never get another chance to visit the Holy Lands unless the Powers-That-Be would send me there.

To quote my dear old Aunt Betty: "Wantin' ain't getting. Ya' gotta' go get it."

Although our operations were ultimately in support of the Israelis, with all of the covert joehootinanny prevalent in that region, we could not gamble U.S. Marine lives and military assets on any of the various factions in Israel knowing in advance exactly where Marine LZs and fire bases would be located. Middle Eastern Security Rule Number One: the fewer people who know about any classified activity, the better the security and the fewer friendly casualties.

By the way, at that time we were up to our giblets in reliable local informers in much of that region, so the U.S. Intelligence folks had their fingers on the pulses of all of those Middle Eastern countries: every darn one of them. However, years later when our blabber-mouthed U.S. Congress spilled the beans about such covert necessities during public hearings in Washington, D.C., our CIA Station Chief in Athens, Greece was immediately assassinated, all of our local informers, every single one of them and often their families as well in Lebanon, Syria, Iraq, Iran, etc. disappeared from the face of the earth and were never seen or heard from again.

When the President of the American University in Beirut, his American faculty, and other Americans citizens in and around Beirut were abducted in July of 1982, we had no reliable snitches, not one, to tell us where to find and extract our people. So much for absurdly pure thoughts and good intentions while mucking around with convoluted Middle Eastern politics.

For crying in the beer, naïve, fudge-headed thinking like that was the main reason why we still had darned little local intel in the months before March of 2003 with which to make the essential tactical decisions before we freed Iraq from Saddam Hussein. Amazingly, the United States had to rely on Egypt, France and Israel for critical pre-invasion intelligence although several of those three had decidedly different goals than ours. If you doubt it; look at the screwed-up results.

Case in point, if we would have had our own on-site intelligence to realize the vast quantities and the critical contents of up to a hundred Iraqi ammunition depots scattered across that barren country, we would have fielded a far more robust invasion force that could have controlled those vast quantities of high-explosive artillery shells, land mines and other antipersonnel weapons. That would have stopped the indigenous warring sects from stealing the thousands of tons of unguarded high-explosive ammunitions with which they made tens of thousands of improvised explosive devices (IEDs) that caused so many of our casualties.

In my seldom-humble opinion, the knuckleheads who reduced the numbers of our combat troops and equipment down to the bare minimum for some jug-headed, pseudo-logical, politically correct reasons are responsible for many of our troops being killed or maimed by IEDs in Iraq.

Back to Beirut where our targeting procedures—as performed by our guys within the city as well as inside and around the local targets themselves—may seem to be almost laughably simple and archaic by today's standards. However, those activities and the now-antique equipment used were classified Top Secret back then, so let's let that old dog lie.

However, in the 1980s when I was a manager on the Multiple Launch Rocket System (MLRS) program at LTV, I talked with Colonel Stewart (later General Stewart) who had been a young officer with a Marine artillery battery that deployed to Beirut in 1957. He told me that because of the targeting coordinates plotted in 1955, our Marine artillery was able to fire-for-effect with first-round accuracy rather than go through the time-consuming, and thus potentially dangerous exercise of bracketing each target with several aiming rounds before firing for effect.

That advantage undoubtedly saved both Marine and even opposition casualties because that unusually quick accuracy had a very discouraging effect on opposing artillery gunners who were still firing ranging (i.e., aiming for accuracy) rounds at our Marines as pre-aimed Marine first-round artillery fires impacted close enough to the opposition guys to encourage them to go home and take the rest of the day off.

Later on the afternoon of the first day, I was riding a bicycle along a narrow, ancient lane to a cluster of mud huts several miles east of Beirut and fairly close to a locally reported but well-hidden pair of opposition 105mm artillery howitzers. As I approached the suspected, small village square—which looked like it was taken right out of the movie "Gunga Din"—I saw a wall-to-wall crowd of local homeboys who were concentrated around a small, wooden stage at the far end of the village square. As my curiosity overcame good sense, I peeked around the corner of an old mud-brick hovel and saw some rough-looking dudes selling people much like African slaves were sold back in the 17th century.

Among the unfortunate people being sold was a light-skinned guy who wore only brief, ragged, short-shorts so that the buyers could see that slave's physical condition. As I took one last look before getting the heck out of Dodge alive, one of the local strap hangers jerked open that slave's mouth with his hands to check that guy's teeth as if he was buying a horse.

Again, this was mid-November of 1955, and within only a few miles east of the opulent luxuries of downtown Beirut, Lebanon; the so-called Paris of the Mediterranean. One never knows, do one? Until full-scale civil war broke out downstream, that sorry book's cover was kept polished and alluring for unwary, naïve tourists.

All I could do was tell U.S. Naval Intelligence the coordinates of that slave market hidden in plain sight within the vast sea of identical mud huts east of Beirut. However, I never heard another word about that light-skinned guy who was sold that day. I often think of that poor guy, even now, and hope that our special operations guys freed him from that miserable situation. If he was freed, very few people would ever know about it; not including me.

As my favorite Italian philosopher, Yogi Berra, once said: "You can observe a lot just by watching."

32. THE "WILD WEST" OF THE MIDDLE EAST

A wild-west-like gun-slingers' shootout in the suburbs of Beirut between opposing Christian and Muslim factions that evening was not only amazing, but very interesting and a bit entertaining. As I passed them on my bicycle, a couple of Christian militia guys with a few of their home boys in tow, and several more Muslim militia guys and their cheering section gathered at opposite ends of one of the hundreds of narrow, cobblestone alleys in the far eastern suburbs of what was then a beautiful, modern city by the sea. Today, much of that is rubble.

I didn't understand what the heck each group was yelling at the other, but it had about the same effect as years earlier when we fish-eating grade-school kids were yelling "Your mama wears army boots" at a gathering gang of antagonistic public grade-school kids back in my low-rent neighborhood in Wichita, Kansas. A blast from the past; I knew that there was going to be big trouble very soon.

When both sides were ready to rumble, one of the Christian militia guys popped out from the safety of a narrow crossing alley and fired from his hip—rather than aiming from his shoulder for better accuracy—with an American-made Browning automatic rifle (BAR) in one long, uninterrupted, 20-round burst. That cat knew how to make a positive first impression. In addition to the lethal stream of 30-06 bullets chewing up the neighborhood, there were brick, rock, baked clay and dry donkey dung chips ricocheting all over the place while the canyon-like echo was deafening.

The moment that the Christian guy fired his last round, he jumped back into the safety of his crossing lane to reload and take a few bows. At the same time, one of the Muslim guys at the other end of that same empty lane popped out and emptied his British-made Sten gun into the same lane from the opposite direction with exactly the same echoing reverberations and lack of lethal effect while women, little kids and old folks hunkered down inside their houses along the lines of fire and only occasionally peeked out as streams of bullets zipped by their front doors in both directions.

While I was watching, those militia guys used up a metric pot-full of ammo between them in their version of Middle Eastern political street theatre, or maybe that was a rite of passage into manhood. Who knows? Later, I heard that the opposing militia shooters and their cheering sections retired to their respective home-boy hangouts to drink a lot of hot, sweet tea and recite the latest chapter and verse of their heroic defense of, or assault on whatever the heck was on their various agendas that day.

Actually, the warring Muslim and Christian factions in and around Beirut had been fussing like the Hatfields and McCoys for a heck of a long time, but with very few casualties on either side. Unfortunately, these same hot heads later discovered suicide car and truck bombs by the Muslims, and high-caliber, more-precise sniping rifles by the Christians. Casualties have soared on both sides ever since.

By the way, Yogi Berra, my favorite Italian philosopher also said that: "The future ain't what it used to be." Yogi was so right.

When talking about classic wild-west shootouts, few sports fans realize that Yogi was a teen-aged gunner on a U.S. Navy artillery barge floating just off shore from the Normandy beachhead on D-Day during the WW II Allied invasion of Nazi-occupied France. Yogi's job was to destroy the Nazi coast-defense cannons; particularly before the Nazi gunners could destroy Yogi's artillery barge. Yogi won. He is still with us. The Nazi cannons and their crews, which were protected by thick concrete and steel bunkers, are long gone. A Baseball Hall of Fame catcher, Yogi was a darn good heavy artillery gunner as well. Yester-years' athletic stars were often real heroes when the brown stuff hit the fan.

33. AIR JORDAN FLIES LOWER.

That same night, after more of our gentlemen intelligence spooks showed up from all across the European and Mediterranean Theaters, my tight-jawed operations around Beirut were abruptly cancelled. That figured because as the only enlisted air intelligence guy in that whole pack of otherwise commissioned intelligence hotshots, they must have considered me the least qualified guy in that whole crew for that mission. Honestly, they were probably right.

That's why I was so darned surprised a short time later when I received further orders from "the Boss" to fly to the divided city of Jerusalem on the same Holy Lands tour that I had not gotten around to cancel yet. So once again, I filled the bill, but just by pure coincidence. However, those orders didn't mention which intel officer would be my fearless leader. Hell's bells, for a complicated rain dance like that operation would be, I'd much rather be the second banana anyway. Like my brother Richard often said: "My momma didn't raise no fools."

Basically, the Boss's orders were to break off from that tour group immediately after arrival, pick-up some prepositioned gear already there, checkout several sites on the ground that had been suggested from high-altitude photos, and if those proved unacceptable, then scour the Palestinian West Bank/Jordanian western desert for at least three helicopter landing zones (LZs)/interlocking artillery fire bases for USMC blocking forces if and when Israel should be attacked by their less-than-friendly neighbors to their north. That was okay with me as long as nobody would be shooting at me or trying to grab me. I had not been issued a weapon to shoot back, and that bothered me more than somewhat when I thought of that light-skinned slave that was sold back in the mud huts east of Beirut

Since I was pretty darned sure that I would never pass this way again, I also planned to kill two birds with one stone. Of course, as a Marine, I would complete my assignment to the best of my ability. However, I promised myself that I would also take every opportunity to visit as many of the Biblical sites that make the Holy Lands so special for Christians, Jews and Muslims. There was no way that I could be in the Holy Land this one time in my life and not bring Mom a stack of color slides to enjoy and, of course, show-off to all of her little old lady friends in St. Anthony's parish. That was quite a challenge, but I figured that I was up to it.

However, several things were initially somewhat troubling. Number one: I thought that Holy Land mission was a two-man operation, but nobody was mentioned to go with me. Say what? And secondly: this initial safari was in the back yard of those bad-assed Palestinian Fedayeen terrorists.

Those murdering bad actors had recently killed four Israelis and wounded ten more at Beit Hanan near Tel Aviv. Somehow, those terrorists got away into the night, which was surprising considering the militant Israelis' reputation. Soon after that, the Fedayeen warned the world that they would commit an even bloodier encore. Bummer. I was unarmed except for a dual-purpose three-inch pocket knife and attached "church key" to pop corks on an occasional bottle of wine.

The next morning as the Air Jordan pilot went through his preflight checklist on our antique, pre-WW II DC-2 transport aircraft, something unacceptable seemed to bug the tall, haughty French pilot who was apparently something of a dandy, at least in his own mind. From his repeated engine run-ups—interrupted by intervals of engine idling and terse but animated radio transmissions to the Beirut airport tower less than 90 feet away—I guessed that he was having trouble with the magnetos which come in handy for safe and reliable aircraft piston-engine operation. Finally, after what must have been about 15 minutes of fussing back and forth on the radio, Frenchy popped up from his seat, stalked out of that antique airplane in a huff, and hurried into the control tower like his hair was on fire. Once there, we could see him arguing theatrically with a dark, swarthy galoot in a badly dated three-piece suit from the 1930's. That could have been his daddy's suit because it darn well was not tailored for him.

A few minutes later, a short, heavy set, fully bearded Arab pilot wearing a bus driver's billed, floppy, "pooper-scooper" type hat balanced on top of his unruly mass of curly black hair came bursting out of the control tower and hurried across the tarmac like the devil himself was after him, literally hopped into our airplane, and added power as soon as his butt hit the pilot's seat. After some of the most erratic tail-dragging, jerky taxiing this side of a Funky Chicken contest, we took off in a kind of porpoise-like mambo that was as jerky as an early 1930s, hand-cranked, Mickey Mouse, nickelodeon cartoon. That was when I began my first in-flight novena.

Later, as we descended precariously low toward the Jordan River, which lay between two ranges of large hills with tiny mud hut villages plastered against the hillsides, my stomach bile was welling up to my Adam's apple when unannounced, at least in English, we suddenly descended to buzz the Sea of Galilei at much faster than cruising speed and a really stupid low altitude of about 50 feet above the water. Thanks to that up-chucking surprise, every passenger onboard that worn-out old puddle jumper became a member of the "Flight 500 Feet Below Sea Level Club."

Personally, I could have gladly foregone that whole fursluggenger flat-hat flyby; at least with that fur-faced, swarthy Arab pilot at the helm and no co-pilot that I could see from my seat in the rear with the gear. Fortunately, ol' Curley did find the Jordanian airport near East Jerusalem where I parted company with a Navy/Marine tourist group (figure 17) and would only see them occasionally until we returned to Beirut and the Sixth Fleet eight days later.

My room in the Jordanian sector of East Jerusalem was on the fourth floor of the King David Hotel. I heard that the hotel had been blown up and rebuilt before I stayed there, and later learned that it was subsequently blown up and rebuilt after I left East Jerusalem. Once again, I had beaten the odds; not by design, but by pure dumb luck.

Like my Marine blood brother, Eladio Gonzalez once said: "Everybody dies. That's life."

Figure 17. Author and Friends Arriving in East Jerusalem

34. YOUNG MO SPEAKS MANY LANGUAGES A LITTLE BIT

My energetic young guide in East Jerusalem and on both sides of the Jordan River (figure 18) was a slim, wiry 14-year-old street-kid named Mohammad, who looked even younger than his sworn "cross-my-heart and hope-to-die" age. Maybe he was. At that time and place, young Muslim kids had to grow up fast and run faster.

Mo claimed that he could speak seven languages including the local Arabic dialect, French, German, Greek, Farsi, English, and when he added a bunch of cuss words to English, he said that was his American lingo. Later, when he added "aye?" after quite a few English sentences, he mimicked me and that became his (and my) soft-spoken version of Canadian; my second language and Mo's eighth.

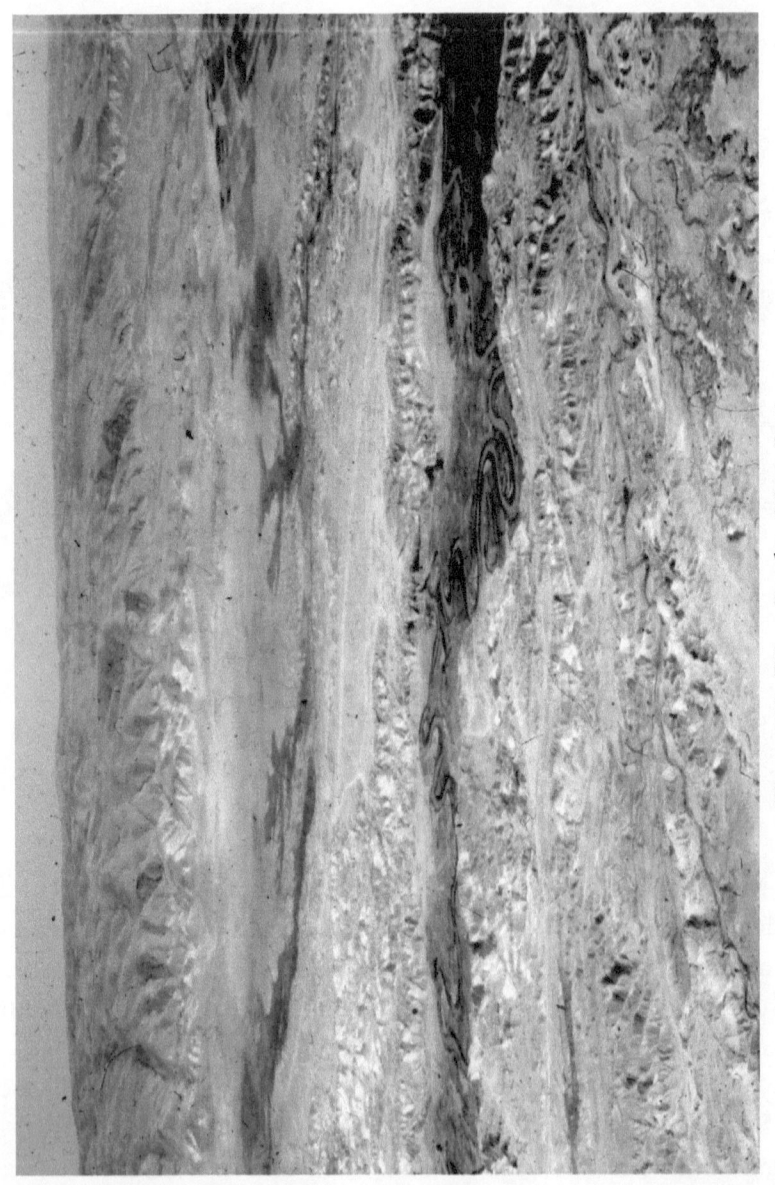

Figure 18: River Jordan Near Jerico

In the narrow alleys like the exotic Street of the Chain (figure 19) where the locals bought and sold fruits, vegetables and fly covered carcasses that looked mostly like skinned, headless cats, Mo seemed to know everybody. He proudly introduced me to many of the street vendors who seemed genuinely glad to see Mo, and welcomed me into their exotic corner of the world, probably because I was with Mo and had quite a bit of folding money in my billfold.

Figure 19. Street of the Chain

Just outside the ancient Damascus Gate (figure 20) in East Jerusalem, I rented a 1941 German WW II Opel Blitz truck that was built for the Nazi Wehrmacht before the United Nations got it after the war and painted the cab blue. Boasting a 75-horsepower straight-six-cylinder gasoline engine and four-wheel drive, that beat-up old relic could have climbed up the Mount of Olives without the luxury of a road. From what remained of the accident-shortened stake bed and the hammered-out wrinkles in the roof of the cab, that old Nazi truck must have rolled over a time or two before that local Arab truck and car rental company received it only one day before I rented it.

Although I had never seen that truck before, I recognized it immediately. It looked exactly as described to me before I left Beirut; right down to the missing glass panes in both doors, the cracked top-to-bottom windshield, the wartime blackout curtains that replaced the missing glass panels, and the gut-shot, two-way, WW II shortwave radio that would never work again because irreplaceable old parts were missing. Only the bottom half of a broken shortwave antenna was still attached to the stake bed behind the cab.

Figure 20. Damascus Gate

An expert radio technician and a lot of luck might not discover that the broken, obsolete antenna contained a new, high-tech antenna connected to a powerful variable-tone transmitter welded into the structure of the truck's alignment frame. That signal was strong enough to permit three or more widely separated receiver stations to accurately triangulate the truck's exact location from far greater distances than ever before. The only control: an ON/OFF switch that looked like something else.

In the vast Jordanian desert wilderness, artillery rich warfare is considerably different than in urban or even rural Europe during WW II. High-explosive, impact-activated warheads are far less effective in desert terrain where they can be instantly buried in the sand before exploding a split-second later. That muffles the explosion to limit the lethal radius and effectiveness of those warheads. However, dense patterns of lethal shrapnel from proximity fused air bursts are far more effective against soft targets such as truck and car convoys, crew-served weapons, encampments, and typical desert animal transportation.

As planned at that time, U.S. Marine artillery with supporting infantry blocking and maneuver forces would be deployed by heavy lift Marine and Navy helicopters at several yet-to-be-determined LZs on the East and/or West Banks of the Jordan River. That forward element of an expeditionary force would engage Jordanian attacks from the east and Syrian attacks from the north by north east. That plan would release IDF units to initially concentrate on potential attacks from Egypt to the west and Lebanon to the north of Israel. Hopefully, quick-reaction U.S. Army Airborne and USAF fighter squadrons could reinforce the Marine land and air blocking forces fairly quickly.

Then why, you may ask, since U.S. Marine forces were preparing to defend Israel from their unfriendly neighbors, would I be scouting around the desert without telling our Israeli friends where the LZs for our blocking forces would be located? To be brutally honest, at that time and in those situations, we just flat did not trust the Israelis to keep that secret to themselves. We would not gamble on allowing the slightest chance that our helicopter LZs would become potential enemy mine fields.

Mo and I spent the first day on the West Bank of the Jordan River, which would be called a stream almost anywhere else in the world; just like the Mount of Olives should be called a large hill, and the Sea of Galilee should have been called a large lake. You would think that our Middle Eastern ancestors would have known better. However, the Sea of Galilee is now called Lake Kinnerret. That's a start in the right direction.

Out in the desert, even on both sides of the Jordan River, I noticed that Mo knew his way around pretty darned well for a city boy. I had no doubt that he had been in those boonies many times before. That evening after we had eaten canned baked beans, canned fruit cocktail, and canned party sausages for our late lunch topped off with Israeli plum jam on crusty Arab flat bread for snacks, at about sundown we stopped at an ancient oases-like well to top-off our fresh water supply. Like Hank Ballard often sang, I figured that we had better "get it while the getting' is good, so good, so good."

Unknown to me, but not to Mo, some of the Arabs living out there were his family, his relatives or at least his friends. As I was breaking a sweat by cranking up a heavy bucket of water from that deep well, Mo disappeared for a few minutes, then returned with the news that we were invited to share a community pot of a thick, meaty stew, then spend the night with an extended Arab family. Mo explained to me that whenever such a generous offer has been made, the Arab offeror would be seriously insulted if his hospitality would be declined. Under those circumstances, and not needing any more tight jaws than we already had, our grateful acceptance was a no-brainer. I did not know what to expect, but I did not want to start off on the wrong foot with the local folks.

Fortunately, I already knew better than to put my best hand, my left hand, into or even near the family stew pot. Essentially, I sat on my left hand to make sure that I could not relax and muck-up my tenuous welcome for good. To the desert-dwelling Arabs, the right hand is the clean or eating hand with which to pluck food out of the community/family cooking pot. The left hand is the "poopy hand" which is considered unclean even when washed with water, sand and/or oil. I understand that if an Arab's right hand is cut off as punishment for some really bad-nasty crime like stealing somebody's goat, that culprit is not allowed to eat directly out of the community stew pot for evermore.

Mo and I did enjoy a quiet but memorable evening. I concentrated on getting acquainted, but as a Canadian photo-journalist from Saskatchewan. Overall, the whole affair was enjoyable, although something like a quiet, carefully reserved evening chat with a family of amicable Mafia strangers back in the United States. I edited every word, spoken or implied, before I said it

By 11:30, we were sleeping comfortably in our skivvies on thick mats on the ground under lightweight but adequate blankets. In fact, I slept better than you might expect that night. I was tired after a long day, and had few worries after Mo explained that when a Muslim man and his family extends their hospitality to anyone, even an infidel like me, that family is honor bound to defend that person against all others with no limitations and no exceptions. I had heard that before, so I decided to go for broke and take Mo at his word or I would not get any sleep at all.

I was flat-out impressed with the code of honor among the Muslim Arabs who lived in the West Bank, and later those on the eastern side of the Jordan River as well. They were honorable people, hospitable hosts, and their women were darned good cooks considering the limitations of their migratory life style.

However, you had better believe that I went back on 100 percent, 360-degree alert as soon as we skedaddled from that camp the next morning. After all, none of the Palestinian Fedayeen terrorists that killed four Israelis and wounded ten more had been caught at that time, and they should have been hiding in that wilderness. Heck fire, we were cavorting around their sand pile collecting information that could be used to defeat them and their sinister playmates someday. I mean, what the heck could possibly go wrong?

When we were passing by the just-emerging walls of Biblical Jericho, I drove out of our way to see those ancient ruins and take a bunch of 35-millimeter slides with my Canon single lens reflex camera as well as some 4-by-5-inch Speed Graphic film plates exactly like I used in high school journalism classes back in 1950 and 1951. I wanted to be able to say that I really did see those Biblical walls (figure 21) as they emerged from so many centuries underground, as well as add to my growing stash of slides for Mom.

Figure 21. Walls of Biblical Jericho Emerge

If we were being watched, and I was beginning to think that we probably were, that also solidified my image as a professional photojournalist working on a future book about Jordan's western desert. It seemed that many in the Holy Lands were eager to attract more tourist folding money, so a book with a lot of pictures would be a good thing for the local economy if the photojournalist was worth a flip. At least that was my story, and I stuck with it.

As we drove around the Jordan River basin (figure 22), Mo pointed out many displaced families of mostly mothers, children and old folks—but few adult males—that were tucked way back out-of-sight in the rolling hills and dunes where they lived in tattered, uncomfortable, flimsy tent communities that were nothing like the large, sturdy, comfortable tents of Mo's friends back at the desert well or the Berbers who surrounded the French air base at Port Lyautey, French Morocco, where our VAH-7 squadron headquarters were based. To me, it seemed that those poor, displaced people were intentionally kept uncomfortable by the tribal Powers-That-Be so as to keep them stirred up, PO'ed, and ready to rumble at any time.

Figure 22. Jordan River Basin

About mid-morning, I noticed a lone Arab rider on a light-gray horse who seemed to be watching us from various distances of about 200 yards up to a mile or more away. As I drove our rented Opal Blitz truck around several higher-ground areas to mislead Mo and anybody else who might be watching, I continued taking a veritable potful of slides and Speed Graphic frames, spinned playful broadies in the sand and had great fun four-wheeling around and over the bases of the dunes where Marine artillery batteries could possibly be laid, but definitely would not be laid. Whenever I looked around a full 360 degrees, I was sure to see that lone horseman somewhere on the horizon. That rascal was definitely still watching us, but at least he wasn't shooting at us.

Late in the afternoon, that Middle Eastern wrangler suddenly reappeared without his horse at a distance of about 80 to 90 yards, aimed his vintage, five-foot long, ultra-slim, Arabian, barn-door action, single-shot rifle at me as I watched him prepare to shoot, and then darned if he didn't take a shot at me. That old-fashioned ball munition with its low muzzle velocity, made a relatively slow but authoritative "whuuush" sound close to my head as I hit the rocky deck head first. If that old weapon had the high velocity of modern rifles, I could have bought the farm for my folks. In fact, at that range I was surprised that he missed me with that very long-barreled rifle, which should have been darned accurate if the barrel and sights were worth a flip, and I would bet that they were.

Since I knew that those vintage rifles were only single shot weapons, I grabbed the M1911 Colt .45-caliber pistol hidden under the driver's seat for just such an occasion, popped back up to shoot before that desert dude could take a second shot, and looked for a sight picture on him. However, he had disappeared behind a pile of boulders somewhat like (figure 23), so I fired seven carefully aimed shots to ricochet around in his hiding place.

Figure 23. Boulders in Jordanian Wilderness

Undoubtedly, that must have put his face in the dirt for a change. My message to him: "I have a lot of ammo, and I am a pretty good shot with a .45-caliber pistol, even at 90 yards." Apparently, that ol' guy got the message loud and clear because he did not show his face or horse again, even from afar.

Since common sense is the better part of valor, I did not cross that 90 yards to checkout my accuracy. Like Marine General James "Mad Dog" Mattis said: "There is nothing better than getting shot at and missed. It's really great."

Like that old Baptist hymn jubilantly affirms: "Count your many blessings; count them one by one." I spent a lot of quiet moments praying while out in that vast Jordanian desert with a local kid who could have been either my friend or my foe depending on the circumstances at any particular moment. The image of that young, light-skinned, nearly naked slave being sold near Beirut was definitely grounded in my subconscious mind. I did not want to be bought and sold.

35. 40MM TARGET PRACTICE ON THE DEAD SEA

For six days and nights, Mo and I crisscrossed the western Jordanian desert at a leisurely pace from the southern shore of the Dead Sea to just southeast of Amman in the Kingdom of Jordan (figures 24, 25, and 26). At each site, I shot a few preparatory 35mm slides with my Canon SLR camera using a standard lens, then a telephoto lens, and often a wide-angle lens with an array of filters to allow me more time to check-out each potential LZ site. Then, we always broke out our big Speed Graphic camera with even more filters, several reflectors, flash attachments, battery packs, tripods, a hand-held light meter and other fancy accessories to take several "money pictures" as if I really was a professional photojournalist working on a picture book.

We never changed our routine from one site to another so that there was no indication that one site was more or less important than another. Then we carefully packed everything away, stowed the equipment in sturdy boxes tied down on the Opal truck's stake bed, ate something, and then moved to our next photo site and did the exact same act all over again.

Figure 24. Shepherds and Desolation

Figure 25. More Jordanian Desert

Figure 26. More Jordanian Wilderness

Bottom line, the potential LZ sites photographed from high-altitude U2 flyovers and studied in precise detail by the U.S. Army's best photo analysts at Oberammergau in Bavaria were spot-on as far as I could tell from the onsite at those locations. I checked the tactical and the geologic characteristics of each of those sites before we were finished, then we continued with our exact routine for quite a while so that not even Mo had a clue what the heck was happening and which locations qualified. Hell's bells, I was sure that he still believed that "Mr. Dave" was a Canadian photojournalist from Saskatchewan.

The last evening before we returned to the King David Hotel in East Jerusalem, I was relaxing at the north end of the Dead Sea while Mo ate yet another whole can of baked beans. He couldn't get enough of that stuff. As I lay mostly on top of that uber-salty water in my boxer shorts, an old Arab gentleman walked down the long incline of the sandy beach about 200 yards out of his way to warn us that we should get the heck off that beach pretty darned soon and take cover because an Israeli gunboat had been coming down there almost every other evening and shooting-up that empty sand beach with its two rapid-firing, twin 40mm Bofers light cannons that are usually used as effective infantry suppression and anti-aircraft weapons. That had to be a whole lot of fun for those Israeli gunners.

I envied those guys for that ideal shooting gallery and all of that free ammunition to shoot. Lord knows that I always wanted to strap on those automatic, rapid-firing, twin cannons and get some quality target time. Sadly, I never got that chance. Bummer.

As we were moving out smartly—the old Arab gentleman did not need to tell us twice—I saw what was probably a similar if not identical Jordanian gunboat headed toward the Israeli side of the Dead Sea, probably to shoot-up one of the Israeli's empty sand beaches just to make some kind of a political or jurisdiction equity statement. That old Arab gentleman mentioned that although those Israeli and Jordanian boats often passed each other on that relatively small body of water, they never fired at each other although they shot up each other's vacant sand beaches with impunity. Go figure.

But considering the powerful, rapid firepower that both of those small boats were sporting, one way or another, when push eventually come to shove, that intense firefight could not last very long. One or the other or both vessels would be blown out of the water mo skoshi, so the intense gunnery practice was neither wasted effort nor wasted ammunition. I sometimes wondered how that matchup finally sorted out in 1967.

36. THE ISRAELI ARMY'S "MAD MOMENT"

Only minutes after we returned that vintage Wehrmacht Opal Blitz truck to the rental dealer just outside the Damascus Gate in East Jerusalem, and had yet to depart the premises, an older, obviously wealthy German gentleman—a self-described collector of WW II equipment—made that same dealer an offer for that old truck which the dealer could not refuse. Later, while debriefing in Beirut, I heard that old relic subsequently disappeared and may not be seen again in that region, at least not in that specific configuration.

When Mo and I finally returned to the King David Hotel, I paid him off and added a generous tip. That kid certainly earned every penny of it, and what the heck, that wasn't my money anyway. Then I morphed into a sweaty tourist-on-the-run mode to gather an impressive pile of 35mm color slides for Mom. In a day and a half, I did my best to get well-balanced color slides of additional Holy Land high points ranging from Bethlehem just down the road to the Way of the Cross, Golgotha, the Garden Tomb and a lot of religious treasures and antiquities in Jerusalem including the huge Muslim mosque at the Dome of the Rock from which Muhammed is said to have ascended into Paradise.

Add to that stack the slides from our safari to Biblical Jericho, Bethlehem (figure 27), the place on the Jordan River where Jesus is believed to have been baptized, the Dead Sea where anyone can lay on the water rather than in the water, telephoto slides of Masada where 960 Jewish rebels committed suicide one night rather than be captured and tortured to death by the occupying Roman army, the salt marshes at the south end of the Dead Sea that cover the sites of Biblical Sodom and Gomora (reference figure 22), etc. so that Mom was sure that I had spent my entire time in the Holy Lands taking various tours and having a grand, leisurely time.

Figure 27. Nativity Church in Bethlehem

Had she known the truth, I feel sure that my Mom would have whispered that news to all of her friends and neighbors before sunset. If so, most of Wichita, Kansas would have known all about that covert operation within 24 hours, and I would be in a heap of trouble. Bless her heart.

One of my more vivid memories is being pinned down about 90 yards around the corner from the Wailing Wall on the wrong end of an Israeli IDF massed-firepower demonstration—what we Marines call a "Mad Moment"—fired into Jordanian East Jerusalem.

After supper, I walked down the hill from the hotel to the west to see and photograph a glorious sunset over Jerusalem. As I arrived at the remnants of some ancient ramparts just above the Green Line, I walked by a Jordanian Arab Legion patrol that was taking a short break by relaxing on scattered ancient blocks of stone. As I paused to light a cigarette, the officer in charge of that patrol made a casual comment and I replied to him in kind. Fairly soon, we were both smoking my Lucky Strike cigarettes and talking about pretty young ladies for some darned reason.

About that time, I noticed that his guys were looking at us soulfully like spanked puppy dogs, so I gave each of those dozen or so Legionnaires a cigarette as well. Pretty soon, we were all smoking my Lucky Strike cigarettes and telling each other flamboyant lies about pretty ladies. Since I could not speak Jordanian and most of the Legionnaires only kind of, sort of spoke a little English—where was Mo when I really needed him—I had to converse more or less in comical pantomime, which was mutually hilarious, but we pretty much understood each other since our minds were tuned to the same station.

After a while, those Jordanian legionnaires had to get back to work, so I returned to the main bar at the King David Hotel for a refill or three. Later, after the last call for alcohol, I decided that I needed a photo or two for Mom of the sublime serenity of the city lights of Jerusalem under a full moon. However, a dense layer of clouds had moved in, which obstructed any photographs of the harvest moon shining over Jerusalem (darn it!), but I would work with whatever I could get.

So I walked back down the hill to frame the best picture of the lights of the King David Hotel with the city lights of East Jerusalem in the background. Well darned if I didn't find that same Jordanian Arab Legion patrol taking another break at the same place as before. So I broke out another pack of Lucky Strikes and passed the smokes around to everyone carrying a rifle.

I was just about to light another cigarette when all hell broke loose. A very loud flash-bang grenade-like explosion jumpstarted the initial massed automatic rifles firing from the Israeli side of the Green Line. That quickly blended with waves of incoming, deep-throated, heavy .50-caliber machinegun shooting so darned intense that it became a single deafening roar in which individual shots could not be differentiated one from the other.

As I tried to get even lower behind a short, ancient stone wall, the Jordanian Legionnaire sprawled next to me casually rolled over and sat up, cradled his World War I British bolt-action Enfield rifle in the crook of his arm and casually leaned back against an ancient 5-foot thick, 2- to 4-foot high, irregular stone wall, lit one of my Lucky Strike cigarettes with a short wooden match as if nothing else mattered, took a long puff, and smiled contentedly at the still-burning match. In the moonless black of night with all of the house lights finally turned off on both sides of the Green Line, that tiny lit match looked more like a freeking flare that would draw even more massed firepower to our tiny refuge.

Already pumped up and swimming in an adrenaline overload, I rolled over as far as I could reach to pinch out that match and just-lit cigarette with my bare fingures. However, I could not reach that contented legionnaire's hand without exposing myself to that veritable surge of ricocheting bullets and sharp-edged rock chips flying around at the speed and with the lethal impact of pistol bullets.

So I laid as low as I could while stretching my right arm to its full length in seemingly agonized slow motion. But I could not reach that potentially telltale glow by only an inch or so while I prayed that I would not hear the distinctive "whump" sound of an American-made, Israeli-launched 81mm mortar round aimed at that tiny flame so close to me.

I know that this is not politically or diplomatically correct, especially since the Israelis are our friends and allies. However, I am sure that if I could have called in a napalm air strike on every one of those IDF guys who were shooting at me at that time, I would have done it in a heartbeat.

After all was said and done, back in the comforts of the King David Hotel, that Mad Moment reminded me of Kinky Friedman's irreverent country music song: "They Ain't Makin' Jews Like Jesus Any More."

Mea culpa, mea culpa, mea maxima culpa with bells on.

37. MISSION PROBABLY ACCOMPLISHED, OR NOT

After piling up a backpack full of unprocessed black-and-white Speed Graphic photographs as well as dozens of rolls of 35mm color slides, according to my mnemonically memorized checklist I believed that my job was finally done. Hey, if someone else with a much better pedigree and/or a lot higher paygrade would follow up after me on the ground and double-check my work, I wouldn't be surprised. In fact, considering my lack of pedigree, I would be surprised if somebody did not double-check my work.

Of course, those LZ/fire bases could then be checked and double-checked again by someone else with an even better pedigree so my initial contributions may or may not have meant boo doodly squat in the overall scheme of things. Nevertheless, with all things considered, I figured that I had given that covert rain dance my best shot, and I would be darned glad to get back to the relative comforts of the Coral Sea.

On my last full day and a half in and around Jerusalem, I made a final whirlwind tour looking for history as more subjects for 35mm slides for Mom. These included the Wailing wall (figure 28); the Way of the Cross (figure 29); Golgotha, the Place of the Skull (figure 30); the Garden of Gethsemane (figure 31); the Garden Tomb which I think is more likely the place where Jesus was entombed rather than the place recognized by the Catholic Church, but that's just me; the Dome of the Rock (figure 32); The Mount of Olives (figure 33) from which I could look down on the whole panorama of the Dome of the Rock (figure 34); with my telescopic lens, the tomb of Kings (figure 35); King David's tower, (the Citidel) by the Jaffa Gate; the pools of Bathezda (figure 36); a whole bunch more shrines and historic places; and the 35mm slides that I cannot find after all of these years. Overall, from the perspective of a young fish eater from Wichita, Kansas, that whole Holy Lands gig just about blew my impressionable mind. Laus Dao.

Figure 28. Wailing Wall

Figure 29. Way of the Cross

Figure 30. Golgotha

Figure 31. Garden of Gethsemane

Figure 32. Dome of the Rock

Figure 33. The Mount of Olives

Figure 34 Dome of the Rock from Mount of Olives

Figure 35 The Tomb of Kings

Figure 36. The Pools of Bathezda

Since I didn't get a heck of a lot of sleep the preceding night and I had been touring on the run all that day, just before sundown, I was relaxing for a moment on my bed in my room when a private firefight erupted across the Green Line divider just west of the King David

Hotel. An older Jewish civilian on the other side of the Green Line, who was armed with a well-worn bolt-action Enfield rifle, was having a slow-motion shootout with an old Muslim civilian who was about 60 feet down the hill below me and about half a block closer to the Green Line (figure 37). That old Muslim guy was armed with some kind of a long-barreled, old-fashioned, single-action revolver—I had never seen one like that before so it may have been a local knockoff—which he struggled to cock with both hands before each wobbly aimed shot.

**Figure 37. Green Line in Jerusalem
(Jordan in Foreground, Israel in Background,
Green Line in Between)**

As I watched that slow-motion mini skirmish without exposing myself to most stray shots, suddenly a long burst of automatic rifle fire—which sounded like an American-made Browning automatic rifle (BAR) concealed in one of the nearby Israeli houses to the west—a string of bullets tracked up the brick and stone side of the King David Hotel and took out both panes of my window in a shower of flying glass shards.

Arguably, that could have been a reasonably unsubtle message that someone was not fooling anybody, and that something even more unfriendly could happen if someone continued to mess around uninvited. What the heck, lingering in that increasingly dangerous neighborhood wasn't on my bucket list anyway. I was more than ready to skedaddle back to the comparative safety of the USS Coral Sea to continue planning for mutually assured destruction between the United States and the Soviet Union.

Only moments later, a blue UN Jeep pulled up between those two old hot heads on each side of the Green Line, the apparently unarmed UN driver wearing a blue helmet climbed out and verbally chastised both of those old guys like slow-learning juveniles until they stopped shooting at each other. With the UN message of peace and love-or-else ringing in their ears, the old Jewish guy went back to raking his tiny yard and the old Muslim went back to painting his front door.

Attempting to be cool, I went downstairs to the hotel bar, ordered a double whiskey and soda, and casually mentioned to the Arab Christian bartender that he probably should tell the Hotel Manager that the window in my former room needed both shattered glass panes replaced. And also, the two bullet holes in the inner wall could be patched at their leisure because I had already moved myself lock, stock and diddy bag into a formerly unoccupied room on the east side of the hotel. Later that day, I heard that my former window was the only window shot out at the King David Hotel that day.

Enough was too much. I cancelled my evening walkabout in East Jerusalem and spent the rest of the evening holding down a bar stool and sampling the chatty barkeeper's wares. Why take an unnecessary chance? Like they say: "Many 'littles' make a hell of a big 'much'."

FYI: A strange thing happened two years later in 1957 when I received a letter at home in Wichita, Kansas from Mo in which he asked me to help him migrate to the United States. Since I was attending Wichita University and living on $110 a month from the G.I. Bill after I was released from the second VA Hospital—that's another story for another time—I could not help the little guy.

The strange thing about that letter was that I did not tell Mo or any other civilian in the Mediterranean theater my full name—just plain "Dave" or "Mister Dave" was good enough—and I sure as heck did not give anyone my home address. Hell's bells, I was sure that Mo thought that I really was a Canadian photojournalist from Saskatchewan working on a future book about the Jordanian desert. Aye.

Do you remember my comments about the raggedy Muslim guys loitering in that back alley when the visiting Navy Intelligence guys first came aboard in Beirut? I certainly did remember, but by the time I received Mo's letter, it was way too late to suddenly get smart. Long story short: our Navy Intelligence guys damn well underestimated the Middle-Eastern Muslim male. That was a bodacious mistake, but here we go again.

38. USS CORAL SEA'S RESIDENT SMART GUY

One balmy afternoon, Si, Guy, Randy, Big Swig and I were relaxing in the shade under the wing of one of our AJ-2 bombers on the flight deck just aft of the Coral Sea's superstructure. All flight operations were cancelled and the flight deck was relatively quiet for a change. The Coral Sea was temporarily at anchor just outside the three-mile limit of Crete while awaiting a storm expected later that day. No one except the Admiral, a few of his friends, and his motor launch crew had gone ashore, and no one was expected to come aboard until the next morning when the Admiral and his crew would return. With a cooling breeze wafting over us, this was one of those uncommon interludes of onboard rest and relaxation, and we were taking full advantage of the unexpected luxury. Life was good on a quiet flight deck.

As we sat on some wooden equipment boxes taking it easy, a tall, slim Navy officer wearing a winter dress blue uniform—although he looked more like a flood victim than a squared-away Navy officer—paced slowly back and forth across the otherwise vacant fantail of the flight deck. That officer's head seemed to be bent down as if inspecting the flight deck just in front of himself, and his fingers were locked together behind his back as he walked. He seemed to be lost in thought as he continued pacing back and forth introspectively for quite a long time.

Curious, I asked my friends if anyone knew who the heck that guy could be, and what the heck was up with his pacing back-and-forth act. One of the guys—I don't remember which one—commented that this

Lieutenant Commander was the ship's resident genius and moody fellow who apparently paced the fantail of the flight deck many times when we were not having flight operations. Apparently I must have been on liberty each time and missed his act until that afternoon.

"Genius huh," I mused out loud. "Gee, does anybody know what his IQ is?" I expected something like 160 out of 161 since 161 was a perfect score back then. However, Guy said somewhat in awe: "I heard his IQ is 142." Amazed, taken by surprise, without thinking I blurted: "Well for crap sake, mine is better than that."

Suddenly, our little group was so quiet I could have heard a nun's fart, and all four of my closest friends in the squadron silently turned toward me in unison and stared at me sort of funny as if I was an alien from outer space. Once again, that and the ubiquitous "PI" (i.e., "Political Influence" notation) displayed on the cover of my personnel folder, and my unexpected, unwanted new job as the one and only Squadron Air Intelligence guru although I sure as heck did not have the proper rank for that job—hell's bells, I wasn't even a commissioned officer—were more grist for the ever-active rumor mill within VAH-7.

To quote my favorite Italian philosopher, Yogi Berra, once again: "Half the lies they tell about me aren't true."

39. AJ-2 MISSION IMPROBABLE

The AJ-2 Savage atom bombers had no machine guns, no cannons, no rockets, no heat-seeking missiles, no anti-heat-seeking flares and no anything else for self-defense. The only armament onboard was the .38-caliber Combat Masterpiece personal revolvers and the occasional .45-caliber M1911 Colt semi-automatic pistols carried by our flight crews in shoulder holsters under Mae West flotation vests.

From the initial operations many moons before, the only real protection for our AJ's had previously been our altitude surprise. The official maximum altitude of the AJ-2 bomber was then posted at 40,000 feet. However, the sneaky little secret was that we could actually cruise right along at 43,000 feet of altitude and possibly be able to squeeze out a bit more if sorely challenged, or if the bomb bay was empty during reconnaissance flights over Iron Curtain countries.

That may not sound like a lot today, but back in 1955, VAH-7 was operating under the best guess that the Soviet's best fighter/interceptor, the early MiG-15, could fly somewhat restrictively at higher altitudes than us on our best day. However, that aircraft could not perform well at that altitude even against our relatively slow, unarmed, whale of an air-to-air refueling tanker/atomic bomber aircraft.

In fact, Yugoslavia gave our CIA a MiG-15 in 1952. According to my friend Navy Commander Roy "Killer" Johnson, who flew that or a similar aircraft at NAS Moffett Field in 1953, the early MiG-15 had dangerous handling faults including difficulty-to-control spinning after stalling, any kind of dives from altitude, and it was not a good gun platform in a dogfight.

One fine day at 43,000 feet over southern Bulgaria, two of our AJ-2 bombers were cruising along while radar mapping their slums or whatever it was that we needed for future contingencies. Suddenly, an early version MiG-15 fighter jet popped around a towering 50,000-foot high cumulonimbus, anvil-headed cloud and made a nerve-wracking identification pass that turned that day and the rest of our days of radar mapping behind the Iron Curtain in the Balkans to clabber. Thank God that obviously rooky pilot made an identification pass before making a game-ending gunnery run on our AJs.

That MiG-15 had two 23mm cannons, one 37mm cannon and maybe even air-to-air rockets, and was among the fastest fighter planes in the world. In the past, the Soviet surrogates in the Balkans could not come up and get us. But suddenly, that MiG-15 negated our operational altitude advantage as it passed above us at 43,500 to 44,000 feet in preparation for shooting down two American atom bombers for violating their sovereignty as well as for flat-out spying. The smoldering wreckage of our bombers and seven dead American bodies would be packed with convictable evidence of those facts.

Both outdated, propeller-driven AJs were toast except for one saving grace; with our wings' fat, laminar-flow aerodynamics, our AJs sure as heck could turn much better than that streamlined MiG-15 at altitude because the aerodynamics of the MiG-15's high-speed, swept-back wings and fuselage airfoils were not designed for aerobatic combat maneuvering in the thin air at 43,000 feet of altitude that they enjoyed at say 35,000 feet. Thank God, ours were.

As soon as the MiG-15 began an extremely shaky left turn on the ragged edge of a steep-turn stall, our AJs made rock-solid controlled right turns and just flew away from that MiG-15 and his sovereign air space because that MiG-15 needed more than a dozen miles at high speed just to turn around in the thin air at that altitude. Looking back over the AJ's tail assembly, that MiG-15 looked like a pig sliding around on ice as it tried to avoid a steep-turn stall that would tumble him down from above our AJs to thousands of feet below.

After our C.O. notified our Powers That Be that we no longer had an altitude advantage at 43,000 feet over the Iron Curtain's smaller surrogate countries so that our one and only tactical advantage was obviously down in the dumper and we were now easy pickings for any Soviet MiG-15s. After a few days of silence, NavAirCom responded that our tactical missions would remain unchanged until further notice. To our fingernail-chewing surprise, that further notice did not happen while we were in the Mediterranean Theatre.

Needless to say, that was not a good time to be assigned to the AJ-2 Savage atom bomber squadrons either there or anywhere else that MiG-15s prowled the wild blue yonder. But not surprisingly, every single member of every single AJ crew in the Mediterranean Theatre saluted and continued with our assigned radar mapping duties behind the Iron Curtain. Flight Skins (i.e., extra pay for flying) are a terribly tempting, addictive motivator, especially if you have a bunch of dependents, or a high-maintenance wife or gal pal.

Somewhere in my many boxes of old 8 mm movies and 35 mm slides, I would not doubt that I still have a short 8mm film clip of that MiG-15/AJ-2 break dance at 43,000 feet over Bulgaria 63 years ago.

40. STRESS IS A BOOGER BEAR.

Late one night as a bunch of us anxiously awaited the last AJ-2 to return to the barn, one of our most senior pilots—I'll call him Commander Lou for obvious reasons—was telling our young Ready Room Talker guy about all of the wonderful things that he had accomplished during his 20-something-year career in naval aviation. The Talker, our most junior enlisted man in our squadron, was happily soaking up all of the details about each commendation and award that Cmdr. Lou had won, how many hours were in his flight log overall and for each particular type of aircraft, how his grown children were all far superior to their contemporaries, his house was better than anyone else's in the squadron, his cars were more expensive, his wife was more accomplished, and other wondrous things like that.

At first, a half dozen other aviators relaxing in the Ready Room were lightly amused to hear that well-liked old "sea daddy" quietly praising himself and his many accomplishments to the new kid on the block. But after maybe an hour of seemingly unending self-adulation, several of the other aviators began to be understandably concerned. You see, the U.S. Navy, like the Air Force, has always been very particular about who could fly their strategic aircraft that could very well carry live atomic bombs over friends and foes, as well as that pilot's state of mind.

All of the aviators in VAH-7 seemed to like Cmdr. Lou, or at least they had made occasional favorable excuses for him. However, this low-key, extensive harangue, just by its nature, had eventually become really problematic to everyone in the ready room that night. The next morning, Cmdr. Lou had a long discussion with the ship's on-board shrink when he should have been briefing for a ten-hour reconnaissance flight at the point of the spear. Suddenly, a new pilot and crew were assigned that mission. None of us knew when or how Cmdr. Lou left the ship while we were cruising under way, but he did.

A few days later, an office pinkie who handled the shrink's paper work, let it slip that Cmdr. Lou had a mental breakdown right there in the shrink's office. He did not want to fly big, vulnerable, cantankerous, tactically obsolete airplanes on and off very short aircraft carrier decks, or over the Soviet Iron Curtain where U.S. aircraft and aircrews tended to disappear and not be seen again. However, he was torn because he could not quit flying; his flight pay made his families' comparatively luxurious lifestyle possible. Without those flight skins, he could not pay all of his bills. As far as flying was concerned, he felt that he had more than used up his share of good luck, and didn't have another carrier-based flight left in him.

I can't say that I blame the old boy. I certainly knew the feeling.

41. WORLD WAR III BEGINS AT SEA?

Late in the fall of 1955, the Soviets were once again rattling their sabers and threatening NATO, the UN, the United States and our allies on an all-too-regular basis. That's what they did best. Apparently, we Good Guys initially paid them no nevermind, but I can't be sure because those strategic-level games were way to heck and gone above my pay grade. However, I did know that if World War III began any time soon, those two Russian subs stationed in the Mediterranean Sea were toast, and VAH-7's atom bombers were in excellent positions to hit our pre-plotted Soviet targets before our two aircraft carriers could possibly be sunk beneath that clear-blue water of the Mediterranean.

That was about 98 percent of our reason for being there. Despite everything else, VAH-7 was ready, willing and able to make mutually assured destruction happen if absolutely necessary.

Sometime in mid-November, the Soviets warned us loud and clearly that if the U.S. Sixth Fleet sailed up the Dardanelles to Istanbul as previously planned to "show the flag" and buy some cheap oriental rugs, they would consider that an unacceptable provocation and the Soviets would unleash the Four Horses of the Apocalypse to jumpstart WW III post haste if not sooner.

Did the average civilians even notice that threat back in the USA? From what I've heard, the answer was not only no, but hell no. I guess our fearless leaders did not want to unnecessarily scare the trousers off any of our civilians before atomic bombs would come raining down on U.S. soil.

So what did our U.S. Navy do about all of that saber rattling? Well, of course, we put all of our naval assets at battle stations, and the Coral Sea Battle Group sailed up the darned Dardanelles to Istanbul with flags flying, swarms of fighter aircraft overhead, and all Naval artillery weapons loaded and ready to fire on a moment's notice. We were, indeed, ready to rumble. However, when operating in the extremely tight confines of the Dardanelles, we would have had a heck of a hard time catapult-launching our three AJ-2 bombers even if their bomb bays were empty.

In my seldom humble opinion, we could possibly catapult launch our fighter aircraft, but only light breezes over the bow, we had absolutely no hope of launching our AJs when fully loaded with atomic bombs. Maybe I was a bit too critical, but that did not seem to be really smart planning, not if the Navy actually believed that the dastardly Soviets were serious that time and we were about one hair-trigger provocation away from mutually assured destruction. On the USS Coral Sea, CVA-43, that was foremost in every man's mind for a very long, gut-wrenching night and day.

At about the same time as our lead destroyer-class ships were arriving at Istanbul harbor not far ahead of us, a Russian mine sweeper sailed out from the Black Sea and into the Dardanelles. That little wooden boat was only marginally bigger than our WW II PT boats—not very big—and had a crew of about a dozen sailors who stood at rigid attention, lowered their naval flag as Passing Honors, and saluted while the massive 14-inch diameter cannons onboard the cruiser Des Moines tracked and bore sighted that dinky little tub as our Coral Sea Battle Group sailed majestically past them.

Fortunately, the Soviets blinked first, darned near everybody breathed a sigh of relief and relaxed, but some did not as the ships of the whole darned battle group went on the normal port-and-starboard liberty schedule—one day on duty, one day off liberty, one day on duty, etc.—as soon as we arrived at Istanbul. The sweet thing about my Squadron Air Intelligence gig was that I often had hardly anything important to do while our ship was anchored and not launching airplanes. Therefore, I could go on liberty every single day rather than every other day like almost every other enlisted guy onboard.

In fact, if I did have some really important tasks that had to be done, that was not enough to keep me off the liberty boats one single day that we were moored in Istanbul harbor. I would bust my backside on the flight deck, down on the hangar deck, and in my office all night if it meant liberty in Istanbul the next day. It was, and I did. I guess that those Turk officials, cab drivers and ladies of the evening were so hungry for Yankee folding money that they did not give two hoots in Hades about the doomsday stash of atom bombs lurking in the bowels of the USS Coral Sea while they were, to quote the Andrews Sisters: "…workin' for the Yankee dollahhh."

42. ISTANBUL'S EXOTIC LITTLE SHEBA'S SEVENTH VEIL

Since the Sixth Fleet had not been to Istanbul for something like four years, the local USO was no longer staffed to entertain our military guys. It was just a big, empty building; a shadow of its former self. However, the wives and daughters of the U.S. Embassy officials volunteered to staff it while we were in town, and they did a great job of spiffing up the joint and making "nice nice" while entertaining the visiting Navy guys and Marines. We appreciated that a lot; bless their hearts and their good intentions.

As my good friend Frank "Si" Simonson and I were returning from an afternoon of rubbernecking around the Blue Mosque and the main bazaar, we noticed that the totally ticked off, obviously embarrassed Embassy wives and daughters were standing outside the USO front door on the main street looking extremely unhappy with palpable dark clouds hanging over their heads while the darndest, wailing, Middle-Eastern flute music and thunderous drum thumping told us that something really exotic was happening inside the USO. So naturally, Si and I hustled inside, but we could not see anything because the main room set aside for dancing was blockaded by the jam-packed backs of what seemed like half of the hordes of Navy guys and Marines in town.

As the thundering, wailing music soared faster and faster, Si and I worked our way through the packed crowd until we could finally see the floor-level stage where an almost cartoonishly endowed Egyptian belly dancer—think Dolly Parton flaunting the last of the original seven veils—had overreacted to our guys' usual mantra of "Take it off. Take it ALL OFF" with enthusiasm unbounded. Then, to everyone's surprise, Little Sheba dropped the seventh veil so that she was totally au natural (at least I thought she was) and gyrating like a whacked-out whirling dervish while a shower of coins and green money continued to pile up exponentially on the stage floor.

Believe me, it is impossible to describe that woman's act, which would not be an appropriate conversational topic for mixed or polite company anyway, so I'm not going to say any more about the devil in the details. However, I would bet that any guy who was there and is still able to sit up and take nourishment, that guy still remembers Little Sheba, the plu-proud Egyptian belly dancer who had curves where most gals don't even have places.

The following day, only a few of the U.S. Embassy wives and none of their daughters were handing out doughnuts and coffee at our thoroughly subdued USO. Apparently someone had circled the wagons and Little Sheba's contract was cancelled at the USO for the rest of our visit in Istanbul. However, I had to work later that night after Little Sheba shed her seventh veil, so I didn't get the news. So the next afternoon, Guy Garafalo and I stopped by the USO again to see who was or was not on the entertainment agenda for that evening.

Did I mention that I can resist almost anything but temptation?

43. "YANKEES GO HOME" IN BODY BAGS.

About 10 minutes after leaving the bridge where the Golden Horn separates Europe from the Middle East, and maybe several hundred yards into the west end of a narrow alley in the maze-like slums of western Istanbul, the low, distinctive clatter of an idling diesel engine—the unmistakable theme song of German automotive excellence—intruded into my subconscious mind. Although not uncommon on the streets of any major city in the world, that sound was disturbingly inappropriate in this extremely narrow, run-down alley in that incredible mass of mazes that forms random clusters of ancient stone and mud brick buildings that were often covered by a thick veneer of something like lumpy stucco. In that fleeting moment between recognition and realization, my pal Guy Garafalo stopped flat footed in his tracks. Something was chillingly wrong, but neither of us knew what the heck it was.

Distracted from our visual search for any unusual nooks or crannies ahead of, and to each side of the darkening, shadow-pocked alley, we both turned, puzzled, to look back over our shoulders along the moldering stone and mud-brick ravine through which we had just walked. As the deepening gloom of the Middle-Eastern twilight slowly enveloped all but the few higher roof tops and minarets, we were amazed to see an antique, black, Mercedes limousine of uncertain vintage try but fail to make a sharp, 90-degree turn into this nameless alley from another much too-narrow intersecting alley behind us. Exceedingly skillful alignment was critical to complete this ill-conceived maneuver on the first try, so the driver behind the darkened windshield backed up and tried again.

"Why the heck would anyone even think of stuffing that hulking bucket of bolts into a narrow danged alley like this?" I asked myself. Barely one car wide, originally intended for horses, push-cart wagons and people on foot, this picturesque but decaying old alley was never intended for any kind of automobile, particularly a luxury-sized limousine from the Bavarian autobahn.

Amused at the eccentricity of whoever was driving that antique limo, I hesitated again as I watched with mounting amazement as the driver backed up again until all but his front bumper and radiator were out of sight beyond the west end of the alley, and were then realigned for a third, more careful attempt at squeezing tightly into the narrow breech between the two furthest hovels.

"That silly clown is gonna' need a whole danged 55-gallon barrel of WD-40 to ram that big hog into this friggin' alley," I mumbled to myself, then chuckled at my own mini-allegory.

Maybe because of the uneven 17th century cobblestone alley, Guy had fallen half a dozen steps behind my impatient lead, and then stopped dead in his tracks.

"That clown has gotta' be flippin' crazy!" Guy said; the amazement in his voice validating what I already knew. Something was wrong, very wrong. Even if that lunatic did get his oversized bucket of precision bolts lined up without scuffing an undoubtedly expensive paint job, he would have barely enough clearance on either side to open even one door of that hulking monster to get out.

"That bozo has gotta' be out of his cotton-pickin' mind!" I agreed.

Suddenly, the more immediately personal aspect hit both of us like a truckload of bricks. With no meaningful clearance to spare between fenders and ancient mud- and stucco-splattered brick walls, not nearly enough safe passage space remained for anyone unfortunate to be a pedestrian at that time and place. In effect, we were staring down a block-long cannon barrel as a tight-fitting cannon shell was breech loaded for launching directly at Guy and yours truly.

As we say in Kansas, we had ripped our britches. Instinctively, we knew that we had messed up miserably and could pay dearly for that mistake. Anyone with even a lick of Middle-Eastern street smarts would have immediately sprinted for safety at the first sight of anything so incredibly threatening; particularly a three-ton Teutonic roto rooter being inserted at the other end of someone's own personal flush pipe. My military "situational awareness" had been asleep at the switch. That tardy realization was almost as distressing as our initial glimpse at impending doom.

Turning around 180 degrees, frantically searching for an escape route in the other direction, both Guy and I quickly verified what we already knew, but did not want to admit even to ourselves. Roughly 80 to 100 yards lay between us and the safety of the next intersecting alley.

"Too far," Guy shouted. "We'll never outrun that big son of a bitch; no way in hell!"

Not a single recessed doorway, nook or man-sized cranny was visible along the unbroken line of deteriorating buildings from where we stood to that distant intersection. Over the hundreds of years that this once-respectable gaggle of low-rent buildings had deteriorated into decrepit hovels, almost all of the windows and doors at alley level had been permanently sealed flush with the outer walls by brick and mortar to discourage transient riff raff and nocturnal burglaries, as well as two desperate U.S. Good Guys looking for a safe haven to avoid being squashed by dangerously inappropriate Teutonic autobahn traffic.

As soon as the massive limousine had finally squeezed its bulk into our scruffy, too-narrow alley, its 12-cylinder supercharged engine immediately revved to a menacing, deep-throated growl as outdated, wide-striped, whitewall tires initially spun unintentionally, then found traction on the irregular cobblestones with an anguished squeal of shrill protest. Simple but effective, the cannon ball from Hell was launched and on the way to make both of us null and void.

Re-energized by the deafening racket, we both whirled back around, looking frantically at the only inset doorway within running distance along the entire lane. However, that sanctuary was at least a dozen yards back toward that rapidly accelerating limousine. Guy and I had one chance and only one chance, but that lay in the wholly unnatural act of running toward, rather than away from onrushing Doomsday.

"Run for that doorway. Back there!" I shouted at Guy just before the lump in my throat choked off all meaningful sounds. Initially slipping on the uneven cobblestones, I frantically dashed toward Guy and the set-back doorway beyond him as the accelerating limousine—now bore-sighting us in the harsh glare of a blinding spotlight mounted dead center on its massive front bumper—screamed like a scalded banshee from Hell. Its sonic energy, surging well ahead of the massive vehicle like an all-engulfing bow wave, reverberated off the ancient stone and mud-brick walls to virtually overwhelm all other physical senses.

For a horrible second or two, which seemed like a heck of a lot more seconds to me, I felt that I was running in slow motion toward an onrushing boogeyman in an incredibly frightening nightmare. Nothing else could be heard over the screaming, thunderous roar of the terrifying monstrosity bearing down on us like the hellish Four Horses of the Apocalypse stampeding side-by-side within that very narrow alley.

With my shocked mind focused way out in front of my body, fixated on the minutest details of the pock-marked, moldering old brick and mortar wall framing the inset doorway beyond Guy—which was possibly the last things I would ever see on the face of God's green earth—I had neither the time nor the agility to go around Guy. So I ran right through him, my 220 pounds taking his 160 pounds with me to safety, barely a split second before we would have become dual radiator ornaments on several tons of onrushing death and destruction.

Seeing that we had beaten that rampaging limo to the only sanctuary in the entire alley, the driver slammed hard on his brakes at the instant he passed within inches of our meager refuge. Immediately, both of his front and back fenders were engulfed in bright sparks as the limo fishtailed against the ancient alley's walls like a hog skidding on ice.

Jammed awkwardly against Guy's backside and the mildewed wall beyond, out of breath and off balance within the narrow doorway, my twisting, overhand throw was more reflex than skill. In the rush of air from the limousine's wake, that lucky throw was hard enough and accurate enough to do the job at that short distance. The impact of an ancient street brick, which I had picked up much earlier as a defensive last-resort, shattered that limousine's rear window with a sharp, resounding explosion like a cannon shot reverberating inside this cavern's walls.

With that, we were out of ammunition. I had used our entire defensive arsenal. But the driver—the dark silhouette of his stylishly long, well-groomed head of hair clearly visible through the gaping hole where his darkly tinted rear window had been—hunched forward and stomped hard on the gas pedal once again to burn twin streaks of acrid rubber down the narrow cobblestone alley. Rear end again fishtailing erratically, his fenders flashed bright balls of flare-like sparks in the gloom as he ricocheted off the old rock and mud-brick walls; first on one side, then on the other side of that ancient alley.

Within seconds, the battle-scarred limousine disappeared around the corner of the wider crossing lane at the far end of the alley in a peal of squalling tires and over-speeding engine, leaving an intermittent trail of black paint scrapings back to our meager sanctuary.

As the occasional vehicles passed by the narrow opening on the far eastern cross road—their bright road lights like flashing strobes momentarily accentuating the faint glow of a single, distant, low-voltage street light—amazingly no one seemed to be aware of the life or death drama that had just unfolded. In their haste to be anywhere else at that gloomy interval between late dusk and total darkness, no one on that distant lane slowed down for even a moment.

"You okay, Dave?" Guy asked, his voice seemingly floating back from the featureless dark shadows.

My ruined night vision mercifully blanked out from the reality of the past few moments, blotting it into a black void hovering as if self-levitated behind a formless mass of swirling fireflies, but leaving a vivid TV-like after-image blur burned into my subconscious memory.

Welcome to exotic Istanbul, ya'll.

44. OLD ACQUAINTANCES NOT FORGOTTEN

The day before that bungled attempted murder by limousine, Francis Goode—a brilliant former high-school classmate who completed the four-year syllabus at Cathedral High School with academic honors, but in only three years—and I bumped into each other at one of the hundreds or maybe thousands of unmarked intersecting alleys in the ancient slum on the west side of Istanbul. What are the odds; how many millions to one? Heck, considering the exact timing, it is more like tens of millions to one for gosh sakes?

If either of us had been a dozen seconds or so either earlier or later than we were, we probably could not have been able to even see the other guy in that dense maze of randomly intersecting mud and brick hovels and alleys. One second, I was all alone as I jogged basically east by southeast while homing on the towering minarets and dome of the Blue Mosque downtown (figure 38), and the next second I bumped into Francis, who was jogging north by north west through the same crumbling old slum.

Figure 38. Blue Mosque in Istanbul

We had not seen each other since the night that we graduated from high school in 1951. "Surprised" is not the word for it. "Incredibly surreal" is more like it. We were both absolutely flabbergasted. Then we had a good laugh about one of the many outlandish tricks that our class comic, Mary Jo Figgins, pulled in high school during our senior year when I was once again an unwitting foil for her whacky sense of humor; usually at somebody else's expense.

Unfortunately, Francis and I could not get together again that night or the next day because he was leaving Istanbul early in the morning on a business trip and would not be back for a week. With no time to spare before darkness would settle in and obscure my only navigational aid—the minarets of the Blue Mosque to the east—we enjoyed another joke that ended with "I resemble that," shook hands again, and each of us jogged off to our separate appointments.

The following evening, Guy and I were almost killed in the same general area by that monstrous German limousine. For many years after that attempted ambush in that ancient, moldering slum, I wondered who the heck would want to squash a couple of fine young fellows like Guy and I.

But then, I also wondered who in the dickens would possibly believe that incredible meeting in that mind-boggling maze was just a flat-out, unexplainable, one-in-a-million coincidence? Heck, anyone who had been there and seen that cluttered maze of stone and brick hovels, as well as the unmarked, randomly meandering, intersecting alleys substituting for actual streets, would never believe that incredibly coincidental meeting between Francis Goode and I was just an extremely unusual quirk of fate.

Whoever that Mercedes driver the next day was, he fairly well ruined at least the fenders and paint job on an extremely well-preserved antique limousine. I hope that failed attempt to squash Guy and I wiped-out that S.O.B's bank account to repair that friggin' Nazi locker box on wheels.

Could that son of a sea cook who was driving that vintage black Mercedes limo have been a Russian agent trying to stir-up another dose of international turmoil after that threatened WW III fiasco? After all, the damn Soviets had threatened World War III if the U.S. Sixth Fleet dared to sail up the Dardanelles to Istanbul. So naturally that's what the U.S. Navy Big Brass, safe in their distant offices in the Pentagon, decided to do. Apparently we peons afloat in the Dardanelles at the point of the spear looked at that situation from a far different perspective.

Fortunately, the Russkies recognized the consequences of all of the sudden U.S. and allied military activities in Europe, the Middle East and Asia. So they blinked first, accepted the muted hints, and then backed off. Good for the Russians. They know all about mutually assured destruction (MAD) from WW II.

But then, maybe that limo driver was a Jordanian Muslim Arab like that guy who shot at me and thankfully missed while Mo and I were out in the vast deserts of western Jordan. Or possibly, he could have been a Turkish intelligence guy who saw that amazing coincidence when I bumped into Francis Goode in that incredible maze by pure coincidence and came to a logical but wrong conclusion.

And what about those Christian and Muslim militias in the dingy, dangerous back alleys of east Beirut, Lebanon? They could have had the homicidal hiccups big time if they knew that I had been in cahoots with the cannon cockers who had been plotting artillery targets in their squalid neighborhoods for future military contingencies.

Hell's bells, that thug in that vintage Teutonic locker box on wheels could have even been one of our dear friends and allies, the Israeli Masada spooks. After all, the Israelis intentionally shot out the windows of my room at the King David Hotel in East Jerusalem; most probably as a not-too-subtle suggestion for me to get the heck out of Dodge and stop bothering them with undiplomatic intel games in what they considered their once and future private sandbox. Of course, they also organized that very impressive firepower "Mad Moment" demonstration when I was with that Jordanian Arab Legion patrol at the Green Line in East Jerusalem. But then again, what the heck, the Kingdom of Jordan could have gotten equally bent out of shape for much the same reasons.

Or maybe, just maybe the bozo in that antique limo was a local hoodlum who wanted to scrape a couple of dead Americans off his radiator just for the pure hell of it. Who knew? The mystery of that failed ambush stayed shrouded in my mind for many years.

At the 2001 reunion of our high school Class of 1951, I finally caught up with Francis Goode for the first time in the 46 years since our incredible meeting in that Istanbul slum. That was the first time that I learned that Francis had indeed been a CIA field agent stationed in Istanbul when we last met.

Voila! That whole fantastic affair became far more understandable than before. I figured that since I was with U.S. Navy Air Intelligence and had just recently returned from playing classified recon games on the ground around those eastern Mediterranean hot spots, and Francis could have been known locally as an agent in the Istanbul CIA office, there was a good chance that one or both of us were being shadowed in that slum back in 1955.

Of course, someone among those previously mentioned "usual suspects" had to have seen Francis and I bump into each other in that incredibly unlikely reunion so far from Wichita, Kansas. Whoever that guy was, he darn sure could not have believed that coincidental meeting was anything but carefully preplanned. Heck, if I didn't know better, I wouldn't have believed it either.

However, on the following evening back in 1955, Francis had already departed for Beirut, where I had been stirring the pot only several weeks before that. Therefore, Guy and I may have inadvertently inherited the thorny rose of retaliation by default. Or, maybe some sinister S.O.B. may have wanted to send a grizzly message to U.S. Naval Intelligence, or the CIA, or the Sixth Fleet, or the United States government, or whoever the heck was a burr under their blanket at that particular time. Of course, that's still pretty much speculation, but now I tend to believe it.

The fact is, I wrestled with that murky mystery in the back of my mind from the fall of 1955 until the fall of 2001 with absolutely nothing to show for it. But now, I think that I may have a handle on it.

However, to complete the circle, it is also possible that unforgettable meeting with Francis in that Istanbul slum was not a coincidence. As a junior CIA spook not privy to the whole story, Francis may not have known the "what" nor the "why" of that situation. From time to time, the notorious senior plotters within the upper ranks of the prior Office of Strategic Services (OSS) from WW II—such as Kim Roosevelt—have been known to jack around with whatever the end that justified whatever the means.

Don't get me wrong, I am darned glad that the CIA was and is on our side. One way or another, those old lethal-game players kept the Soviet KGB off balance, as nervous as long-tailed cats in a room full of rocking chairs, looking back over their shoulders 24/7, and wary of their own shadows. Make no mistake, that was most assuredly a darn good thing for our side.

However, the Devil was in the details. Rest assured, there were still a few dedicated old-school zealots in the CIA who would give nasty, sneaky bastards a bad name.

45. FORCE 10 (?) STORM AT SEA

There are few more dangerous jobs than working on the flight deck of a U.S. Navy aircraft carrier, or anybody's aircraft carrier for that matter. All day and through half of the night, many highly trained, dedicated, hard-working men are swarming over the flight deck in all kinds of weather. During launch and recovery operations of fixed-wing aircraft, the aircraft carrier turns into the wind, which could easily be blowing at 30 knots an hour or more, and the ship can cruise at 30 knots or more, so the combined wind over the deck can be 60 knots (about 68 miles per hour) or even somewhat more.

During the engine prelaunch run-ups of both jets and propeller-driven aircraft, the biggest dangers are being chopped to death by ubiquitous aircraft propellers, or being sucked into the air intakes of jet engines, or even being blown off the flight deck and into the water 70 feet below, especially at night. All that and more happens too often on the flight deck.

Recovery operations—when the aircraft are landing and being moved away from flight operations—involve ever-lurking lethal dangers that range from breaking woven steel recovery cables that snap, whip around and cut unwary deck personnel to pieces. These cables have the power to cut cleanly through the titanium afterburner at the tail of a jet fighter like hot butter with an animal skinning knife. If the unmanned aircraft are temporarily located on the forward flight deck and a landing aircraft breaks past the tennis-court-net-like steel cables of the Davis barrier, all of the aircraft located forward of that barrier—which are often already fueled and armed for the next launch—tend to explode, burn things and hurt people.

The last time I saw the USS Ticonderoga on the Mediterranean Sea, it was burning from bow to fantail about a mile off our port side. We knew that sailors and Marines were dying in that holocaust. Thank God, all of our VAH-7 guys on that ship survived, but many other guys onboard the Ticonderoga were not so lucky.

May God have mercy on their souls.

The noise on the flight deck is deafening so that many communications must be done with hand signals because even when nose-to-nose, a person's words often cannot be understood let alone distinctly heard, and the ear protection to muffle the incredible racket also muffles conversations as well as shouted warnings, orders and replies. You don't want to make a mistake on the flight deck. And then, all of these problems are exacerbated during night operations when, for wartime training purposes, there is no general lighting on the flight deck. The danger is so intense that those working on the flight deck must not be exposed to normal incandescent lighting before venturing out on the flight deck. Therefore, the ready rooms and maintenance operations leading to the flight deck are illuminated only by red lights at night so that no one will lose their night vision before going out onto the very busy and very dangerous flight deck during flight operations.

We don't usually see the casualty lists, but fatal and maiming accidents are not uncommon on U.S. Navy flight decks, day or night, good weather or bad. I cannot say enough about how impressive all these flight deck guys (i.e., the magnificent "deck apes") are as they work in all kinds of weather, all kinds of light or lack of light, and in all kinds of dangerous operations.

All catapult launches, flight deck launches and recovery operations can be incredibly stressful for flight crews. However, their most frightening moments can be just getting to and from their aircraft while walking on the flight deck, especially at night. As often said, aircraft carrier operations involve many hours of routine procedures interrupted by moments of sheer terror and sudden, excruciating pain.

Late one evening during a more intense than usual storm on the Mediterranean, I was snookered into volunteering to go out on the pitching, wind- and foam-swept flight deck to begin tying down one of our bombers because that responsible plane captain and his maintenance crew were nowhere to be found despite repeated calls over the ship's PA systems. That job had to be done, but the choice was between the only three people in Ready Room One at that time. That included our X.O. (a commander), Lt. Weigle the bombardier/navigator and me. So naturally, there really was no choice at all. A "can do" attitude was not only expected, but highly appreciated in VAH-7. We got things done when no one else was available to "get 'er done."

I had just attached the third or fourth of eight heavy duty tie-downs on an AJ-2 bomber that was located a little more than 150 feet aft of the ship's bow, just in front of the USS Coral Sea's superstructure, and 70 feet above the water in good weather; which this wasn't. Suddenly I had a premonition of an onrushing deadly mass of unstoppable power behind me, then almost immediately sensed before I actually saw that a huge, dark, ominous shadow looming over my left shoulder like Dooms Day was about to knock me off the flight deck.

Instantly that gigantic black mass turned into a huge wave that had broken over the plunging ship's bow and slammed me against the

AJ's starboard main landing gear as the other four or five heavy steel tie-down sets disappeared over the starboard side of the ship in a surge of white water that could have taken me and the AJ with it if the first three or four tie-downs that I installed were not securely fastened.

Mark up one saved, damned-expensive, atom bomber for ol' Dave. Spitting salt water and snorting it out through my nose, I desperately held on with both my arms and my legs wrapped around the landing gear shock absorbers as the pounding white water nearly gave me a wild ride overboard into the hereafter. No one could have missed me until far too late to save me.

Thoroughly soaked despite my foul weather gear—as well as my chest pretty much bruised and battered from being smashed so hard against the AJ's main landing gear shock absorber—I abandoned that darned AJ to its fate. Hell's bells, I was fresh out of tie downs anyway, so I sprinted to the superstructure's inboard hatch before another wave could pound on me where there were no arm or leg holds to save me. Returning to Ready Room One looking like the mythical Davy Jones, I was ready to take names and kick butts.

There, I refreshed the newly arrived plane captain's memory—he outranked me by a lot, but I backed that bozo against a bulkhead nose-to-nose and called him everything but a white man while the XO removed himself from the ready room so he would not be a witness—about why the heck he received monthly flight skins (i.e., pay to fly) for not flying very much.

Within minutes, that plane captain and half a dozen or more of those marvelous Navy flight-deck-apes, each wearing flotation devices, flight deck foul-weather gear, and joined together by life lines, were all over that bomber like white on rice as they did the tie-down trick correctly that I had so foolishly tried to do all by myself and for the first time. Let's hear it for the flight-deck apes/wizards. I love those guys and the admiral should too.

If we are lucky enough to live through our stupid danged mistakes, sometimes we can learn from our stupid danged mistakes. Case in point: I have never picked up an airplane tie-down since that night. That's a good start anyway.

46. AJ-2 BOMBER'S TROUBLED TACTICS

In the event of World War III, each of our bombers was pre-assigned a primary and a secondary target or two behind the Iron Curtain. If the red flag ever went up and our three bombers launched off the USS Coral Sea, and the second three bombers were launched off the USS Ticondaroga—all six carrying their Mark-15 atom bombs—probably none of them would ever return to the 6th Fleet even if their missions were successful. Our chances of getting to our assigned far flung targets in our relatively slow (471 mph), unarmed AJs were slim on a standard day against a MiG-15 (624 mph), just a little bit better on a dark and stormy night, but never very good. However, even if we did succeed in obliterating our targets, our AJ-2 bombers could not carry both that massive atom bomb plus enough fuel to return to our ships or, in most cases, even to friendly territory in Europe.

In my seldom-humble opinion, these were borderline suicide missions to distract and decoy the enemy so that they would change their order of battle, thereby giving the USAF better chances to hit their targets with their faster, higher flying, high-tech atom bombers like the Boeing B-47s and the B-52s. In that case, no matter how many AJs and flight crews would be lost, the Congressional appropriations for a stop-gap Navy carrier-based atomic strike force could be considered by some strategic tacticians as money well spent. However, the flight crews had a different prospective.

For example, think of the Battle of Midway in WW II where all of the slow US TBM aircraft of Torpedo Squadron Eight were shot down by the faster, well-armed Japanese Zero fighter planes at low altitude as they made their futile sea-level torpedo attacks. Only one TBM pilot, Lt. Gay, and none of the crewmembers of Torpedo Squadron Eight survived that unprotected attack. However, their sacrifice cleared the higher altitudes of the Japanese fighter aircraft that descended to sea level to attack the TBM aircraft. That allowed our following dive bombers to decimate the Japanese fleet essentially unopposed, and made possible our eventual victory over the Japanese in the Pacific Theatre to win WW II. God bless Torpedo Squadron Eight.

For the VAH squadrons, our World War III missions could be like Armageddon on steroids. All of our flight crews knew that if we actually did get through the many defensive wickets and destroyed our Russian targets, then we would invariably run out of fuel, bail out, and the Soviet home-defense forces, farmers, and other irritated local folks along our routes of return would be hunting us with revenge in their hearts and minds. After we attack Mother Russia, those people would undoubtedly be very hard to get along with if we should live so long as to find out. You could not blame them.

In a hot war or a cold war, we will fight the way we train. Training a carrier-based atom-bomb strike force is no simple matter. First, our strike force is best evaluated if they temporarily believe that they are actually in WW III. That takes a lot of coordination with our allies, the other military elements in the region, and even with the potential enemy itself. In effect, our high command had to tell the Soviets that we were actually training on a certain day to obliterate them in WW III. That was essential so that the Soviets could do things like inform their two submarines in the Mediterranean to go hide on the bottom of the Aegean Sea among all of the islands for about 12 hours so that our Anti-Submarine Warfare (ASW) forces would not inadvertently "practice" by actually sinking some of their seagoing assets or shooting down some of their aircraft. Friend and foe communications were essential for realistic but safe practice wars.

On the USS Coral Sea, only a handful of people knew that this training exercise was not the real thing. As the acting VAH-7 Air Intelligence guy, I knew the real story but I could not tell anyone. In fact, I was not really sure if even our Commanding Officer knew whether this was the real thing or not. I think that he may have known, although I could not bring up the subject and talk about it without making a serious security Boo Boo. Of course, our C.O. had the security clearance, but I did not know if he had the ubiquitous need-to-know. I did my job and he did his, but neither of us knew what the other guy knew.

All three of our AJs were fully prepared to carry out their war-time missions. I had to brief all crewmembers on a new pinwheel point at which to start their long-range bombing runs—we did not want to show the Soviets where that actual pinwheel location was, or they would be waiting there for us during a real war—, our primary and secondary targets, our radar tracking to and from the primary and secondary targets, and code language to redirect to alternative targets or terminate the missions. That was a biggie when we were playing war games with real, live atom bombs, as was the A-bomb arming/disarming check list that I prepared back in Pax River, and a bunch of highly classified chores like that. I was as busy as a one-armed man in a wallpaper hanging contest.

While I was briefing the four crews to prep and fly our three AJ's, the first AJ was located over the elevator doors that opened on the flight deck to transfer an actual Mark-15 atom bomb into the bomb bay of the first AJ to launch. A fully capable/qualified crew included a standby pilot who warmed up the aircraft so that it was ready to go when the first briefed crew stepped onto the flight deck. For all purposes and intents, these bombers and their crews were going to war, and they would not be coming back no matter whether they were successful or flubbed the whole mission. The dreaded red flag of WW III had finally gone up, and each man did his duty to the best of his abilities. Go Navy. Semper fi.

In the scramble to launch, I don't remember who was in the first AJ to launch except for my good friend, Guy "Ginny" Garafalo. After I finished briefing all four crews including our backup crew, I walked Guy to his fully loaded bomber idling on the catapult and ready to launch. Guy knew for certain that no matter what happened, an actual mission would not end well for him. He knew that he was probably a dead man walking. But my always dependable, fun-loving little buddy did not hesitate for one second. He had trained for this moment, he was ready to do his duty, and he put one foot in front of the other until he was at the AJ's hatch. We shook hands and he said something like: "It's been good knowing you, Dave" and I replied "Right back at ya', good buddy." Then, without another word, he crawled into the hatch of his bomber and went to work to save America from our nasty, damned Soviet enemies.

Our first AJ was in the air headed east to our new target pinwheel and our second AJ was loaded with a second live atomic bomb and sitting on the catapult during the final engine run-up when that training exercise was finally cancelled. We did not need to take the same chances with another real Mark-15 atom bomb being launched, and then needing a hazardous carrier landing to keep from reducing our inventory of atom bombs, bombers, crew members and aircraft carriers. All systems were "GO" and worked precisely as practiced many times before. Guy's AJ was called off with a coded message from the Coral Sea, and the two fighter planes accompanying them also relayed the message as well to make sure that everybody received the message to terminate the mission.

The dirty little secret: if the first AJ did not receive the abort message from the Coral Sea or as relayed from the fighter escort and had then entered Soviet air space, if all had turned to clabber and the fighter planes could not keep the AJ from continuing with its bombing run ala the movie *Dr. Strangelove* ("Yee haaah"), as the very last resort, the fighter escort was ordered to fire across the AJ's nose. In the extremely unlikely chance that the AJ did not abort and return to the Coral Sea, the unthinkable would become reality.

The gist of this story: don't judge a book by its cover. When the flag went up, those easy going, fun-loving, party pals like my friends Guy Garafalo, Si Simonsen and Big Swig Swigonski were as tough minded, determined and as heroic as any warriors that I have known. If you were their enemy during WW III, they would do their best to kill you, your family, your friends and your livestock for the sake of God and country.

By the way, none of the flight crews or anyone else—maybe not even our detachment C.O.—knew that if WW III actually became a reality, each AJ could carry four rather than three aircrew members as a backup to ensure that the Mark-15 atom bomb would be properly armed and delivered on target as directed by that 16-page check-off instruction that I prepared while under armed guard back at Pax River. If it went that way, the bombardier/navigator from the spare crew would be the fourth man in the first AJ launched, and the third crewmember from the spare crew would be the fourth man in the second AJ launched from one carrier. The air intelligence pogue would be the fourth man in the third AJ launched. Since my boss, Lt. Ed, was no longer with us, I would have won that dubious honor by default. The many hours spent with the Mark-15 documents and mockup would have earned me the opportunity to buy the farm somewhere deep behind the Iron Curtain for God and country. Lucky me.

Since the AJ-2 bombers did not carry enough fuel to bomb their targets and then fly back to friendly territory anyway—and don't forget the swarms of MiG-15s defending Mother Russia—the extra crewmen could be the backup to ensure that the bomb could be properly prepared and double checked to detonate as intended.

With apologies to Waylan and Willie, sometimes when night flights were over and aircrews were enjoying their last cigarettes and coffee in the squadron Ready Room, you might have heard a chorus or two of "Mamas, don't let your babies grow up to be AJ aircrew."

47. CHEAP BERETTA PISTOL

Back in Genoa, our occasionally wayward friend, Randy, wanted to buy a cheap Beretta pistol to take home to Jersey City, New Jersey as a "souvenir." Yeah, right! That, of course, was a highly illegal transaction for both the buyer and the seller in Italy. However, Randy found an Italian street kid who promised him that he would bring a Beretta pistol to a dingy, out-of-the-way waterfront bar on our last day in port.

Since the transaction had to be under the table in a booth in the back in a corner in the dark rather than up front in full view where the cops might see something and interfere, Randy put a $10 bill on the outside of his money roll and about 10 or so one dollar bills inside the roll so that his money roll looked like the $100 that the street kid wanted for his pistol rather than the $19 or so that he was actually going to get.

I wish I could have seen the sly looks on each of their faces during the actual transact6ion between those two slick operators as the street kid passed the gun under the table to Randy with one hand as Randy passed the $100 (actually $19) under the table to the street kid's other hand. The deal "done and did," both slick operators left the bar in a hurry and in different directions to avoid being arrested or rolled by the other guy's friends.

Back at a booth in the back in a corner in the dark of a fairly respectable bar on the main drag, Randy was still chuckling about how he had slyly short-changed the silly street kid when he discovered that his newly purchased Beretta pistol had no operating mechanisms inside it. And don't you know that scene was repeated when the Italian kid discovered that he had only $19 and not $100.

Don't you just love the synergy when a couple of similar sly minds get together? What goes around comes around.

48. THE BIG FLOATER: A 24/7 CARD GAME

The "Big Floater" was a ubiquitous poker game that continued uninterrupted for 24 hours of each day, 7 days of each week except for General Quarters, Man Overboard and fire drills, the occasional crash and shipboard fire, and other serious rain dances like that. While the ship was underway at sea, the game seldom ended. The players were constantly rotating in and out depending upon their work schedules; think of the *Guys and Dolls* movie and Nathan Detroit. At any time, four to six guys were playing, a half dozen more were kibitzing and kidding around with each other, and all were listening to the uninterrupted country/western classic music from a 45 rpm record player that held a dozen or so records in a single stack.

When all had been played, the stack was manually turned over and we listened to a dozen or so "B" side country/western records. When that was completed, the "B" sides were again turned over to play the "A" sides again, etc., etc. You get the picture.

Gambling for money was forbidden on U.S. Navy ships, so worthless poker chips were used to keep track instead of money. The dirty little secret was that the chips could actually be converted to a dime, a quarter or half a buck each if you knew the going rate, who was the current banker, and where the bank was located. The bank never ceased to pay off like clockwork, so the better/luckier poker players went ashore with pockets full of ready whip-out. The losers usually went ashore with extra packs of cigarettes hidden in the ankles of their sox, but mostly just to rubber neck if they could not arrange reasonable payday loans.

Centered in the enlisted men's break room of Marine Squadron VMS-222 (the Checkerboard Squadron), the Big Floater accommodated any enlisted man in any onboard squadron. If you wanted to try your luck, you were welcome at the table if you had the ready whip-out money to play. Once in a while, the game had to move to accommodate unforeseen contingencies, but it always returned to its home base at VMS-222.

By the way, I never did discover how in the heck they painted that black and white checkerboard design on those roundish engine cowlings and flight helmets. At least one of their guys must have been a spray-painting wizard.

While in Istanbul, Si and I found a record store that featured classical records. So we went in and I bought "The Nutcracker Suite" in a set of two 45-rpm records. The first night out at sea, we stopped by the Big Floater for a couple of hands of "Dealer's Choice." While Si kept the gaggle busy at the table by calling tens, twos, fours and one-eyed jacks are wild and several other silly games like that, I turned over the exhausted stack of country/western records and swapped out two well-worn records for the two new Nutcracker Suite records in the stack. Then I eased on out the door to get some overdue shuteye while Si won a new pair of shoes for some future unborn baby.

I really doubted that many if any of those rough and ready deck apes, grease monkeys, red-shirted armorers, etc. had ever heard any classical music in their whole cotton-picking lives, and double doubted that even a few, if any, would go for that music when it intruded onto their never ending stack of country/western music. But when we returned to the Big Floater the next day, we were surprised to hear the Nutcracker Suite playing loud and proud, and even more surprised to learn that those guys liked it so much that they were playing both records over and over again. But the real surprise was their favorite of all of the tunes: "The Dance of the Sugarplum Fairies."

Line dance to that, y'all.

49. PAY DAY HEIST

While operating at sea well beyond the sight of land, the entire cash payroll (normal pay, hazard duty pay, flight pay, etc.) for the 3,500 officers and enlisted men aboard the USS Coral Sea was stolen. It was onboard under lock and key, and then it just disappeared. The onboard search of the ship was immediate and intense with SPs and MPs looking into every personal locker, aircraft, dark corner, dirty clothes sack, bunk, locker box, equipment box, etc. No one went ashore as we sailed right by the beautiful and enticing Isle of Rhodes.

I had a heck of a time in the Air Intelligence offices complex because I had a potful of safes loaded with Top Secret information and four-drawer files full of lower classified material. But everything had to be opened and inspected by the ship's security personnel who had to have both the appropriate security clearances and the ubiquitous Need-To-Know. This was as serious as a heart attack, and nobody was immune. "Sorry about that, Admiral, the Chief of Naval Operations specifically said 'everybody'."

At first, the ship's Captain announced over the PA system that the culprit had better return the money ASAP because there was no way that big bundle of folding greenbacks could remain undetected under such intense scrutiny within a single ship. But after about five days, we knew that the bad/nasty thief had made good his nefarious scheme when the ship's chaplain announced over the PA system that we should all pray for the poor misguided souls who had stolen that huge amount (and volume) of green folding money. Finally, the Sixth Fleet replaced the money dollar for dollar and we had a long-overdue payday, but we never did get back to Rhodes. Darn those nasty thieves!

Several months later, one of the junior Navy fighter pilots was apprehended with all of that money after his plane landed and was inspected in the United States after a short over-water flight from the homeward-bound USS Coral Sea. We also heard that the pilot's plane captain was also busted. His feeble alibi didn't hold water because there is nothing about a plane captain's sole responsibility—his one aircraft—that the plane captain does not know about, especially something as large as a couple of sea bags full of green folding money. 'Taint possible. But of course, you could have said the same darn thing about those crooks ever getting their grabbers on all of that moo-lah in the first place.

So much for all officers being honorable gentlemen.

50. U.S. MARINE QUOTE

"A Marine is a Marine. I set that policy two weeks ago. There's no such thing as a former Marine. You're a Marine, just in a different uniform, and you're in a different phase of your life. But you'll always be a Marine because you went to Parris Island, San Diego or the hills of Quantico. There's no such thing as a former Marine."

General James F. Amos, 35th Commandant, U.S. Marine Corps.

V. GOING HOME THE HARD WAY

1. THE AJ-2 FACTOR

As mentioned before, the twin-engine AJ-2 Savage, the U.S. Navy's only carrier-based atom bomber in the winter of 1955, was a flying hydraulic leak. Whether parked on the aircraft carrier's deck or cruising at 43,000 feet above the blue Mediterranean Sea, I cannot recall a single operation that did not include at least one significant leak in the AJ-2's hydraulic-actuated systems that essentially controlled that aircraft.

That was one of the reasons that the AJ-2 required at least 12-manhours of maintenance work for every hour of flight time. Since our average missions were usually 8 to 12 hours in duration, that equated to approximately 96 to 144 hours of maintenance work on each of our bombers aboard the USS Coral Sea in order to be ready for the next flight operation. When all three bombers were airborne, that could equate to about 288 minimum man-hours up to 432 or more man-hours of maintenance work to be mission ready for the next flight operations.

Of course, that just flat could not be done even if every maintenance guy in our detachment worked around the clock. However, the missions were defined and loosely scheduled by The-Powers-That-Be somewhere in the rear with the gear, so they were launched anyway as short-handed and deficient as the maintenance had to be.

Needless to say, our squadron's morale was lower than whale dung in the deepest part of the Philippine Trench, and there was zero relief in sight until we returned home. Our maintenance guys were almost always exhausted, and our flight crews were as jittery as long-tailed cats in a room full of rocking chairs.

2. BROKEN ARROW

That mission-critical workload overload may or may not explain why one of our three bombers was temporarily parked unattended and not yet tied down with adjustable steel cables by the plane captain and the ship's efficient deck apes on the flight deck. Suddenly the ship turned hard to port (i.e., to the left) and the weary old AJ slid on a big patch of its own super-slippery hydralube fluid and fell off the flight deck onto a 40mm Boffers anti-aircraft gun tub (figure 39)on the starboard (i.e., the right) side just forward of the ship's main superstructure (figures 40 and 41). With its backbone spar and wing spar both boogered beyond repair, we were all hoping that the old junker would catch a strong breeze and just tip on over and fall into the Mediterranean Sea to disappear into the depths so that we would not have to mess around with it any more.

Unfortunately, we had no such luck. The next thing we knew, a gaggle of the ship's boson mates and deck apes swarmed all over it and tied it down in the gun tub so that all of our hopes were dashed. Those guys can really tie a pot-full of gnarly knots in no-time at all.

Figure 39. AJ-2 Atom Bomber Up Close in Gun Tub

Figure 40. AJ-2 Atom Bomber, Distant in Gun Tub

Figure 41. 40 MM Gun Tub

Actually, we could not allow the darned old bomber to sink gracefully down to Davy Jones locker in the clear blue Mediterranean Sea. The reason, the Russian sub that always shadowed our battle group in that sector undoubtedly knew what had happened and would surly mark the spot where our bomber sank. Soon, a Soviet "fishing trawler" would recover it some night, and turn it over to their intelligence pukes who would check it out and then report that the U.S. Navy's AJ-2 Savage bomber was a pitiful excuse for an atom bomber that would be easy pickings for any of the thousands of MiG-15 aircraft in the Soviet Union's inventories. That was another Top Secret that we did not want to divulge.

To make matters worse, the entire squadron was preparing to go back to the good ol' USA two days later, I believe, on 19 December, just in time for Christmas. After seven months of day and night flight operations, often over and around Russia and several of the Soviet Union's Iron Curtain countries, every guy in the entire squadron was more than ready for well-earned R&R (i.e., rest and recuperation) stateside.

Back home in Wichita, Kansas, my folks were planning one of our family's best dual celebrations ever. The boxes of Arpege and Shalimar French perfumes from Beirut, Lebanon; carved cameos from southern Italy; ornamental throw rugs from Istanbul; rosaries and crosses from Rome; and beautiful cedar wood carvings from Bethlehem had all been hand-picked and sent home early. Their pre-wrapped packages had already arrived at 254 South Poplar and were undoubtedly piled under the decorated tree awaiting Christmas morning.

3. CLASSIFIED JUNK

Two days later, our two remaining bombers on the USS Coral Sea launched on the first leg of their long flights back stateside, and all of our maintenance and support guys got off the ship somewhere in the western Mediterranean. I think that's right. I was up to my giblets in work on the busted AJ, highly classified documents and equipment, transferring security accounts and like that so I was too darned busy then to remember now where a fleet of MATS (i.e., Military Air Transport Service) four-engine DC-6 passenger aircraft was waiting to whisk them back to the USA in time for their pre-approved Christmas holidays.

The only evidence that Squadron VAH-7, Detachment 31, had ever been onboard the USS Coral Sea was one permanently boogered AJ-2 atom bomber and yours truly. Someone had to stay aboard the ship to process what was left of the broken bomber at the US Navy facility on an Italian Naval Base just south of Naples, Italy. Since I was the only Air Intelligence guy in the squadron after my boss broke his leg in that unauthorized, forbidden, murder cycle wreck in downtown Palma, Majorca, I got the cotton-pickin' rose right up my nose. Sometimes, I'm just lucky that way.

Because we had an array of big bad-nasty atomic bombs stashed deep in the bowels of the USS Coral Sea, our ship was not allowed to approach within three miles of any port in the Mediterranean except Gibraltar, which was a heavily armed British military base at that time, and those wacky Turks at Istanbul who apparently did not give a flip about total destruction as long as we arrived with plenty of Yankee dollars to spend. However, there were no sea-going cranes large enough to cherry pick an entire atom bomber out of a gun tub about 62 feet above the water line on short notice. Thank goodness that the Italian government and the US Navy huddled, scratched each other's backs, and finally agreed to make an exception just that one time. Lookout Naples, here we come.

Giddyapp.

4. MAGNIFICENT ITALIAN CARAVAN

About mid-morning, the giant USS Coral Sea, atom bombs and all, snuggled up against the undersized civilian dock at Naples as what seemed like every street vendor, cab driver, pimp and hooker in town awaited an unscheduled boon while every shop owner in town was undoubtedly replacing their normal price tags on their displayed products with the twice as expensive price tags featured when the US Navy's 6th Fleet sailors and Marines were turned loose on the town.

Within about two hours, our fatally broken bomber was lifted off the USS Coral Sea and placed on the biggest darned trailer that I have ever seen. I think the darned thing was used to move houses or maybe a couple of main battle tanks at one time. Whatever its purpose, that was an incredibly big rig with dozens of "dually" wheels and extra axles fore and aft

As soon as the broken AJ-2 was tied down with its outboard wings and vertical stabilizer folded for transport, a U.S. Navy truck driver and yours truly drove about a dozen miles south to a huge secluded hangar at a U.S. Navy facility on a sprawling Italian Navy base beside the main road to Pompeii and Sorrento.

Fore and aft, we were escorted by a caravan of several dozens of Italian motorcycle cops and two Italian armored personnel carriers as scores of sirens wailed their macho warnings, civilian traffic horns bleated their macho replies, and the various Italian motorized units seemed to constantly challenge each other to be the lead element in that grand but unscheduled parade. I guess it was a matter of competitive Italian pride. Whatever, that grand mêlée was a magnificent sight to behold.

After inventorying almost every inch of the wreckage and signing a whole slew of forms in triplicate or even worse, I found myself the only passenger in a U.S. Navy jeep hightailing it unescorted back to the Bay of Naples where, hopefully, there would be some kind of transportation left behind to ferry me out to the ship. A motorboat or small helicopter or Italian water taxi or even a rowboat would be just fine with me.

But surprise, surprise, when we got back to the dock, there was the huge USS Coral Sea aircraft carrier waiting patiently at the dock with onboard sailors and a flock of local ciao bellas—"ciao" means "hello" and "goodbye" in Italian—yelling futile sweet nothings back and forth although there would be no port-and-starboard or any other kind of liberty that day.

When I walked up the Coral Sea's gangplank all alone in my dungarees and saluted the quarterdeck, a gang of bosons mates immediately cast off all of the cinch lines to the dock, tugboat horns bellowed their harbor supremacy, and a whole gaggle of sailors lining the flight deck and catwalks aboard the ship turned to the next guy and said: "Holy cow! Who the heck is that guy?"

5. 21 DECEMBER 1955

About mid-morning the next day, the Coral Sea was cruising the required three miles off the shores of Cannes on the French Riviera, but there would be no unscheduled liberty call for the ship's sailors and Marines that day either. Instead, a search-and-rescue helicopter lifted off the flight deck with just one passenger aboard, yours truly, with my liberty uniform, my sea bag, obligatory chest-pack parachute and harness, and travel orders with a top-notch travel priority written and signed by Admiral Ralph Ofstie on his own personal stationary and enclosed in his matching personal envelope with ornamental crest. Bless his heart.

As we landed at Cannes where a big MATS four-engine R4D—that's a DC-6 in the civilian airliner business—was waiting at the engine run-up pad at the end of the runway with all four engines idling and fully ready for takeoff. As I walked toward that big bird, the aft passenger door opened and an enlisted guy in a Navy/Marine flight suit came down the ladder to check me out before allowing me to come aboard.

Basically, he had to know how much I weighed (about 220 pounds), the same about my sea bag (about 60 pounds) and my mandatory parachute chest pack which weighed something like 20 to 30 pounds if I remember right (heck, I don't know anymore). He checked my orders and my travel priority, then checked it again, rolled his eyes and said "Wow! Are you some kind of buddies with the Admiral or what?" Caught off guard, the only thing I could think to say offhand was "Isn't everybody?" Wanting no further conversation that could hoo-doo the whole rain dance, I left him standing there wondering what the heck and talking to himself.

That airplane was so full of cargo—mostly Christmas presents for loved ones back home—that it was packed to its weight and balance limits. So they had to offload approximately 310 pounds of cargo onto the tarmac runway to satisfy the space and weight specifications for me and my gear. I hated to see all of that Christmas stuff offloaded onto the end of the runway just to accommodate me, but I really wanted to get home for Christmas. So I kept my mouth shut and looked the other way. Like that old country song says: "We had a long way to go and a short time to get there, cha, cha, cha."

That evening about sunset, we landed at Port Lyautey, French Morocco, after a fairly sporty hop over the storm-wracked Mediterranean Sea; visually avoiding several lines of towering, lightening-lit cumuli nimbus clouds that boiled up from the relatively warm air of the North African deserts to collide with the seriously cold winter air coming down slope from the frozen Alps. Some of those big-time weather systems were undoubtedly piled up well above 50,000 feet in altitude.

Turbulence like that could easily chew up and spit out even a big four-motor transport plane, so we logged a bit more than an extra hour of flight time by going around it along the Costa del Sol of Spain. We had no chance to fly over those winter weather systems, and even less chance of getting any sleep while the reliable old R4D bounced around like a cork in a maelstrom. Ride 'em cowboys, and don't even try to go to sleep! "Nevvah hotche, gringo hitch hiker."

Port Lyautey was the end of the line: the most westerly stop on that MATS R4D's weekly loop around the Mediterranean Sea. With destinations like Cairo, Amman, Tehran, Jerusalem, Beirut, Istanbul, Athens, Rome, Madrid and other pretty neat places in between, who would not want to fly a tour or two with MATS in the Med? You talk about a dream tour of duty; that would be it. As y'all know, if you want to run with the big dogs, you have to get the heck off the front porch.

6. 22 DECEMBER 1955

After a decent supper in the aircrew mess where rare treats like orange and tomato juices with ice cubes were usually on the menu, I finally hit the sack a little after midnight. Four hours later, a sailor shook my foot and asked me if I would like to take the next flight to the US. All I needed was really high-priority travel orders and the moves to be on the flight line in uniform with the mandatory parachute within 30 minutes because the westbound MATS R4D bird was taking off in about 40 minutes. Fortunately, I had all of the prerequisites and even bummed a couple of cups of "black plasma" coffee from the flight crew during the pre-flight engine run-up. I guess I looked like I really needed a caffeine injection.

As the sun rose over the golden topped minarets of Rabat on our starboard side and the fog-shrouded Rock of Gibraltar straight ahead, we all relaxed and enjoyed the dazzling view as we began a leisurely climbing left turn and headed for the good old USA on the other side of the Big Pond. Pumped up, I still had an outside shot at being home for Christmas. That prospect was enough to keep me stoked and in the game.

Soon after we passed the point of no return between the British Isles and the Azores, the number three engine overheated and began running fairly rough, so the co-pilot shut that sucker down and feathered the propeller. Lajes in the Azores was the closest military airport so we went for it although that little outpost in the middle of the Atlantic was not the best place for an unscheduled liberty call. Like they say: "No matter how hot or cold, foggy or stormy the weather can be during the day, there was absolutely nothing to do in Lajes at night."

One of the sportier airports in the civilized world, as I remember the Lajes' skimpy runway had a fairly sizeable mountain rising from one end of the runway, the wildly surging surf of the winter Atlantic Ocean was pounding on the other end of that runway, and there was not a heck of a lot of runway concrete in between. Everyone onboard that hobbled old workhorse crossed his fingers and/or prayed for an east-to-west (or was it west-to-east?) landing pattern so that we could request a straight-in landing rather than a drop-in over that hulking mountain. I remember something about offering up my first born to be either a Franciscan monk or a Sister of St. Joseph if we could just land safely.

7. 23 DECEMBER 1955

The next morning, I was enjoying the luxury of a hot, leisurely, no-time-limit shower while finishing my five S's when one of the MATS crewman stopped by to tell me that a couple of engine magnetos and other stuff had been replaced overnight, and we could be good to go in about an hour. Although the crews of most touch-and-go air traffic at Lajes ate their meals out of khaki sacks, we were treated to real eggs any way we wanted them and all that we wanted, bacon galore, and mounds of hash browns just off the griddle with buckets of hot coffee and orange juice to wash it all down ("What, no grits?"). Once again, I was stoked. Christmas in Wichita, Kansas, was an outside possibility if the Good Lord was willing and all four engines kept cranking along.

Our flight to Norfolk Naval Air Station in Virginia was uneventful. But by the time that we got there about a dozen hours behind schedule, every military aircraft that was going someplace for Christmas had already flown the coop. With no more free flights from Norfolk to Sanford Naval Air Station in northeastern Florida, I had to wave my magic travel orders from Admiral Ofstie to get a spare stewardess' jump seat on an otherwise fully loaded civilian airliner from Norfolk to Orlando, Florida.

Who knew that a Sixth Fleet Admiral way to heck and gone over in the Mediterranean had that much influence with civilian airlines back in the real world? Not me, that's for sure. But every time I needed to show my travel orders, a door opened and I was on my way again.

Funny thing, when I boarded that civilian airplane with my parachute under my arm, the airline folks got all bent out of shape about me carrying a parachute onboard their airplane. Even though I explained to them that I had just flown on two MATS versions of their civilian but identical DC-6 airplanes, and that both military flight crews had insisted, yae demanded that I have a parachute before they would let me onboard their R4D/DC-6 airplanes. However, Delta Airlines—or was it United Airline? I forget—would not allow me onboard their DC-6 airliner with a parachute under my arm. Say what?

Of course, I lost that discussion, but I did make a lame excuse by mentioning how I could be confused by the conflicting requirements for identical aircraft. But they insisted again that I stow my parachute in the cargo hold. Heck, I was tired of toting it around anyway.

When I finally checked in at my new duty station at the Sanford, Florida, Naval Air Station that evening, I called Mom and Dad and told them that I was safely back in the states, but all of the military aircraft that were going toward Wichita were long gone, and all of the civilian airliners were booked solid so there was no chance of me getting a hop home for Christmas. It was a darned shame, but I had given it my best shot, yet could not domino. Much like when I crashed, burned and nearly drowned in the swamp off the main runway at NAS Sauffley Field, I had ran out of air speed, altitude and ideas; all at the same time.

Incidently, that phone call home was the first time that I had spoken to my family or anyone else in the United States since VAH-7 departed from the United States for operations in the Mediterranean Sea. Today's readers—who are accustomed to instant communications by cell phones, smart phones, Skype, eMail, etc.—find that lack of communications hard to understand. I had tried to make phone contact back home several times, both onboard the ships and in a dozen ports, but had failed miserably.

Aside from major emergencies, that service was not available even when ashore. A letter took about a week to get home to Kansas, and my family's letters took about a week to get from the USA to our ships at sea. We thought that was a pretty darned decent time line. However, if not for the old, WW II TBM aircraft that delivered our mail while we were underway at sea, those letters from home would have taken a heck of a lot longer to be delivered.

8. 24 DECEMBER 1955

Early the next morning as I ate breakfast in a nearly deserted chow hall, I became somewhat but understandably hyper and decided to give it one last shot just for the pure heck of it. So I put on my winter service dress uniform, packed a small gym bag with just the bare essentials, walked out the gate and headed west down a secondary road across Florida toward far-away Kansas.

I was going to give myself one last chance although the odds appeared to be slim and none. Luckily, I had sent all of my Christmas presents home from the Mediterranean before the first of December, or I would have been dragging my large sea bag just to tote my bare essentials.

I believe that I walked only about a mile or so west along that secondary road when a local farmer in an old Chevy pick'em-up truck stopped and offered me a ride. He asked me where I was going, and then told me about an Air Force Base less an hour west from there. Since he said that he had nothing else to do that morning, he gave me a straight shot from his half pint of pop skull from within his bib overalls, drove me to that airbase, let me off at the gate, and then turned around and headed back east because his original destination turned out to be pretty close to the place where he first picked me up.

That old boy was certainly spreading the Christmas cheer, bottled and otherwise. God bless him.

At the AFB base gate and then the Flight Operations Line, I showed them the golden high-priority travel orders that I received from Admiral Ofstie on the Coral Sea off the coast at Cannes, France, which I probably should have surrendered back at NAS Sanford. However, in the confusion, I didn't. The Operations Officer read my travel priority, shook my hand and said that the only flight that they had going west was an old World War II B-25 bomber that was headed for Dallas, Texas, and that I was welcome to fly on it. I figured that Dallas was a heck of a lot closer to Wichita, so I took them up on it. I had never flown in a B-25 before, and looked forward to the unusual experience.

We took off before noon and headed for a quick stopover at the infamous Tampa Bay AFB—of "One (airplane) a day in Tampa Bay" fame—on the west coast of Florida. That was a blessing because the essentially unmuffled exhausts on B-25 engines made a racket inside the aircraft that was mind numbing. While the flight crew were doing whatever Air Force flight crews do at their stopovers, I headed for the PX and picked up some ear plugs to muffle the racket. As I was leaving the PX, I met a Navy pilot and co-pilot who were headed for Hutchinson, Kansas, in a twin-engine P2V patrol aircraft. Since Hutchinson was only about 60 miles west of Wichita, and Dallas was a heck of a lot further away, I opted to switch my ride to the Navy P2V, another airplane in which I had never flown before.

So I went back to the flight line to get my gear and tell the Air Force flight crew goodbye, Merry Christmas, and thanks a lot for the ride. When the B-25 pilot asked me where I was headed, I told him that Wichita, Kansas, was my final destination. The pilot nodded a couple of times and huddled with his co-pilot for a moment. Then he offered to fly me directly to Wichita's McConnell Air Base. He swore that they would still have plenty of time to get back to Dallas for Christmas.

To save time and paperwork, he changed our flight plan after we were at cruising altitude. What a great guy! I owe him and the copilot a lot. I owe them the happy ending to this sea story.

We landed at McConnell Air Force Base a little after 8 p.m. I could not thank those guys enough, but I tried. Then I called home and Mom asked me where I was spending the night before Christmas. I told her that I was just about 10 miles away at McConnell AFB and was ready to be picked up whenever they could get around to it. Mom and Dad met me at the base main gate, and we were home at 254 South Poplar and singing Christmas carols at 10 p.m.

9. 25 DECEMBER 1955

That was one of the most memorable and enjoyable Christmases ever.

10. ADMIRAL OFSTIE'S GOLD-PLATED TRAVEL ORDERS

Funny thing; I never did read Admiral Oftsie's magic, gold-plated travel orders. Granted, they got me a priority helicopter ride from the USS Coral Sea to the airport at Cannes, France; priority rides on two MAT's aircraft even though both crews had to adjust their critical weight and balance calculations to accommodate me, and one of them had to offload the weight of me and my gear in high-priority Christmas cargo that was already on the aircraft when I came onboard; the ride on the already fully loaded commercial airliner from Norfolk to Orlando, and the Air Force B-25 bomber flight to Dallas, Texas, that diverted all of the way over to Wichita, Kansas so that I could be home for Christmas Eve.

Thank you so much to everyone who contributed to those wonderful memories. I can never repay you, but I will never forget you.

Actually, the most amazing perk was when Delta Airlines—or was it United Airlines, I forgot—who initially told me that they had no space on their flight from Norfolk to Orlando, but suddenly found an empty stewardess's jump seat for me after the guy in charge of ticketing had second thoughts, asked for and read my travel orders from an admiral he probably never heard of on the far distant Mediterranean Sea.

Who'da thunk that an admiral's travel orders would mean boo doodly to a commercial airline? But they certainly did. Whenever I needed a boost to get through the next wicket on my way home to my family in time for Christmas, I pulled out Admiral Ofstie's magic envelope, handed it to whoever was in charge of that particular function, and it never failed to grease the skids to move me on down the line toward home.

Crazy or not, I really did not want to read the Admiral's travel orders at that time. I guess I did not want to break the spell, so I saved it for later. That one page sheet, neatly folded in the Admiral's personal letterhead envelope, worked like a charm. It never failed me from Cannes, France to Wichita, Kansas. Having been born superstitious, possibly due to the distant Irish side of our family, and brainwashed by 12 years of parochial schooling, I did not want to hoodoo whatever the mojo that did not let me down. Of course, I would love to read it now, but that magic document is long gone so I will never know what kind of a sob story Admiral Ofstie wrote that made a bunch of good people jump through hoops for an insignificant pogue like me so many years ago.

I'm guessing that the admiral probably thought that I had volunteered to do the intricate, extensive, really difficult process and signoff tasks to decommission that Top Secret AJ-2 atom bomber out of the goodness of my heart so that VAH-7 squadron's Air Intelligence Officer could be free to go home to be with his family for Christmas. Admiral Ofstie obviously did not know that I was just doing my job.

11. LT. MILLSAP DOMINOED.

Lt. Millsap was a senior Naval Aviator who moved up from the black-shoe, blue-water Navy to the aviation branch of the Navy many years before I knew him. Basically a low-key, high-efficiency guy, he was a big-time pain in the neck for not only the maintenance crews, but also for his own flight crew. He was as picky as a guy who picks fly crap out of a pepper shaker, and he always insisted that everything on his AJ-2 bomber be done exactly as specified in "the Book."

However, that was the reason why he and his crew were still alive. Lt. Millsap allowed no cutting of corners or deviations. His prefight checkouts were marvels to behold as he checked and rechecked every aspect of his bomber's operational systems that had already been checked and rechecked by our hard-working maintenance guys and his personal plane captain, who was also a top-notch nitpicker in his own rite. It seemed that everyone on the hanger deck and the flight deck hated to see Lt. Millsap coming; everyone but me.

I knew that he was a meticulous, highly qualified, senior command pilot who reviewed all of our aircraft squawks and practiced all emergency procedures over and over again while most other pilots usually just tested any such procedure a few times, read the literature, and made a few mental notes. Ever since I was a Boy Scout, and reinforced by my Marine training, I was committed to being prepared for any contingency. I was sure that he would be more prepared than most pilots to preserve my hide in an aerial emergency. Lt. Millsap was my kind of guy from cat-shot or deck run takeoff to a solid landing on even the worst pitching flight deck on the darkest night.

I remember one exceptionally stormy night at about 2 a.m. in a heavy sea when he persisted for eight passes on the tossing carrier deck before the LSO (i.e., Landing Signal Officer) could finally guide him safely back onto the flight deck. Afterwards, while debriefing in the Ready Room, Lt. Millsap was as cool as sliced and iced cucumber bits. That was just another work day in six degrees of freedom for that old guy

We were all quietly proud and somewhat relieved that we had not lost an AJ-2 bomber during flight operations on our overseas deployment. No one wanted to say anything that might hoodoo our luck, but then that last-minute SNAFU (i.e., "situation normal; all fouled up") in the gun tub blotted our record just before we headed west across the Big Pond to the good old USA.

Then, somewhere between the Azores and the U.S. east coast, Lt. Millsap's bomber was cruising along at about 35,000 feet when all four airmen onboard heard three rapid, very loud bangs and then, to their horror, they saw their whole starboard engine, nacelle and propeller fall off into the foam-topped Atlantic Ocean thousands of feet below. The bombardier/navigator and the third-crewman later told me that they knew for sure that they were going to get dunked in that freezing winter storm below and probably get dead when their AJ-2 would ultimately turn into a submarine. That damaged, heavily loaded aircraft could not make it all of the way to a safe landing on one engine.

That is, they were scared spitless until a split second later when they felt and then heard the J51 turbojet in the AJ's tail roar into full-throated operation. Normally shut down except for some launch operations from the carrier deck or a bit more speed to aid tactical maneuverability, that turbojet engine had been almost miraculously activated. The normally closed hydraulically actuated air-inlet door to the turbojet engine had been suddenly opened, possibly by the last drop of the hydraulic power just before the turbojet was started and took over the propulsion function of the just-departed engine and propeller. Almost miraculously rejuvenated, that wounded old AJ-2 bomber hobbled home and landed safely.

As the bombardier/navigator and my third-crew friend later swore to me, Millsap analyzed the problem in a split second and automatically performed the emergency turbojet airway intake-door opening operation before the airway intake door activation system lost all hydraulic activation power. If not opened by then, the air inlet door to the turbojet could not be opened, the jet would not be able to start, and the whole crew would have gotten very wet or worse in the freezing Atlantic Ocean. So although we did lose one bomber over the side during the entire deployment, we counted our many blessings; we counted them one by one, and then relaxed because our overseas tour for 1955 was finally over.

12. SAVING ME FROM MYSELF.

About two weeks before I was discharged early to play spring football at DU, the squadron C.O.—not my former shipboard detachment C.O., but the overall squadron C.O. who still looked a lot like Elmer Fudd—he waved me into his office one morning, jollied me around kind of like a concerned father to his rudderless son, and then promised me that if I would accept his generous offer to re-enlist for another four years, he would guarantee me that I could fly as the third crew on the new whiz bang twin-jet replacement atom bomber; the sleek, much faster, higher flying Douglas A3D.

That decision actually took me about a nanosecond to process and reject in my mind, but I let it drag out for about a day because he seemed to be so sincere. I do believe that he thought that he was doing me a huge favor. Like: what the heck else was I qualified to do in the civilian world anyway? I think that he was trying to save me from myself.

Actually, that conversation was a good omen to me because it was pluperfect proof a'plenty that he had not figured out what I had been doing on the side in VAH-7 instead of accepting active duty as a staff sergeant stateside in the Marines. That was also proof positive that our detachment C.O. on the Lake Champlain and then the Coral Sea did not have a clue about my primary assignment or he would have spilled the beans to our squadron C.O.

Funny thing, I am sure that at least some of the enlisted men, especially the flying third crewmen, pretty well had me pegged, but only to the level of whispered scuttlebutt. Who ever heard of an enlisted guy performing the function of the Squadron Intelligence Officer unassisted, or any of that other unusual stuff that had happened? But I don't believe any of the officers, not even Lt. Weiglie with whom I spent a lot of time in Rome and elsewhere, ever connected all of the dots.

Over those nine months of reporting to Naval Air Intelligence on the side, I never praised Captain Fudd for his inspirational leadership or for anything else for that matter. He probably meant well, but as far as I could determine from far distant Detachment 31 at sea, he did not rate a whole heck of a lot of kudos, so I almost never mentioned him in my reports. But wouldn't you know that old ring knocker was promoted to admiral about a year or so later. He must have done a lot of things right, but those were only known well above my pay grade. Anyway, the word never got down to me.

Like the old country classic goes: "Here's a quarter, call someone who cares."

We did not know then that the next big whale (the A3D Skywarrior) was not an overall improvement in the Navy/Marine racetrack landing pattern which had caused AJ crews so much anxiety throughout the Navy. Not only that, but the A3D's only entry/exit hatch was on the bottom of the fuselage, which made it a real widow maker even when it splashed in shallow water or landed with its wheels up. Also, the A3D did not have a crew ejection system although the Air Force version of the same bomber, the B66 Destroyer, did have a crew ejection system. Go figure. Then, if you can, please explain all of that to me in simple terms that even I can understand.

Very soon after VAH-7 transitioned from AJ-2 Savage bombers to the A3D bombers, that designation became commonly known by the aircrews as "All 3 Dead" instead of A3D because very few crewmembers would survive any of the accidents in which aircraft were lost on the deck or on the water. Although I never had anything to do with VAH-7 after I danced out the front gate in February, I will bet you a dollar to a dime that every time those A3Ds landed on an aircraft carrier, Vultures' Row—that elevated catwalk around each aircraft carrier's superstructure—was crammed with amateur paparazzi photographers, all hoping to get a photo of an A3D disaster to sell to Time Magazine.

Personally, I never thought that the Navy's slice of the Congressional budget for aerial delivery of atom bombs was worth the loss of all of those good men. They were truly heroes of the Cold War. They made a big difference in our free world, but very few outside their immediate circle knew that.

13. AJ-2 CRASHED IN THE SANFORD CITY DUMP.

About a week before I boogied out the Main Gate for good, I was taking it easy in the base control tower watching flight operations over a mug of coffee and a Danish sweet roll when the massive steel bolt that held an AJ-2's vertical stabilizer—the vertical part of the tail assembly—sheared while that bomber was approaching the landing pattern. This bolt allowed the vertical tail assembly to be folded to fit within the tight confines of the aircraft carrier's hanger deck during shipboard maintenance.

Right away, the AJ's massive vertical stabilizer began repeatedly slamming against one of the horizontal stabilizers—the horizontal parts of the tail assembly that control upward and downward flight—as the bomber approached NAS Sanford, Florida in the landing pattern. It was gut check time for that flight crew.

After both the bombardier/navigator and third crewman bailed out at that very low altitude—I watched both jump and prayed intensely until I could see white silk deployed at the last second, and then in thanksgiving for saving their lives—Lt. Radtke radioed the tower and said that he believed that he could "land this darned bird." A former Navy test pilot at NAS Pax River, Radtke was said to have ice water in his veins, and was generally considered by most to be the most proficient pilot in the squadron regardless of rank. Therefore, everybody in the control tower just naturally went along with his evaluation. If anybody could do it, Lt. Radtke could do it.

However, as he entered the base's racetrack landing pattern at the first 90-degree turn at an altitude less than 1,000 feet, the vertical stabilizer went bonkers, the bomber flipped over on its back into an unrecoverable inverted "split S" dive toward the ground so close below. Amazingly, Lt. Radtke popped out of his seat, ran back on the cabin's ceiling, dove through the already open escape hatch, and pulled his ripcord just in time for the parachute to activate and stop his lethal fall at only a minimal altitude above the ground.

Lt. Radtke was a very cool character whenever the fit hit the shan. When he jumped out of the rescue helicopter back at the control tower, he trotted over to the grass and kissed the ground, then nonchalantly walked into the debriefing room as if nothing life-threatening had happened. That man really was a legend in his own time. When he talked about flying, I listened and so did many of the flying personnel with VAH-7. Lt. Radtke was, indeed, a very special pilot who we all believed would go far in Navy Aviation.

The AJ-2 bomber crashed inverted in the middle of the Sanford City Dump and exploded in a big ball of fire and ugly black smoke. Burning and distorted parts were scattered over a radius of hundreds of feet. In fact, Si told me many years later that it took almost a month for the squadron and accident investigation personnel to sort through the city dump and separate the blackened and distorted bomber parts from the blackened and distorted old bicycles, refrigerators, auto parts, trash cans, tin cans and other twisted worthless junk.

That reminds me once again of the advice given to Royal Air Force (RAF) pilots during WW II: "When a crash seems inevitable, endeavor to strike the softest, cheapest object in the vicinity as slowly and gently as possible." Unfortunately, sometimes that is not an option.

14. DOOMS DAY ALARM

Just days before I left the squadron, the C.O. asked me if I would help to ferry a number of atom bombs to a classified offshore destination. I thought about that for about a nanosecond, and decided that I had pushed my luck much too far already. I did not want to overwork Holy Joe, my guardian angel, any more than necessary. I am sure that he needed some R & R too.

If the truth were told, I did not have one more flight left in me. So I gave up my ride to the new intelligence officer who really wanted to see that destination from the foldout seat of a U.S. Navy atom bomber. However, I did think that I should lend a hand in the operation as a gesture of something or other, so I helped to load a live Mark-15 atom bomb into the belly of one of our AJs, double checked the loading and safety procedures, and certified that all was hunky dory with Bubba the Bomb as far as Squadron Air Intelligence was concerned. Then I eased on over to the base control tower to have yet another cup of free coffee and watch them take off in relative comfort.

After the mandatory pass on the Compass Rose for this type of mission, the AJ lined up at the end of the runway for takeoff after a flawless engine run-up and checkout. However, with the tower binoculars, we could see some kind of an intensive discussion going on between the pilot and the bombardier/ navigator with added comments from the third crewman as well. Suddenly, without any radio contact, all four airmen—the pilot, the bombardier/navigator, the third seat crewman and the new guy who had hitched a ride on the auxiliary jump seat—scrambled out of the bomber and ran away from it as fast as they could run with helmets and attachments, harnesses and all of that flight gear still hanging on their bodies. If it was a footrace, I was betting on the third crewman to win by his large snozzola, but the new guy took the lead and held it.

Amazed, we watch them run a fairly decent distance, possibly a city block or so down the taxiway like as if they were chased by the rabid hounds of hell. But then, they all stopped, bent over and sucked wind almost as if choreographed as a group exercise, then looked back at the bomber as if they were waiting for something to happen. After that, they huddled for a moment while a flight line truck popped out of a hangar and headed their way. Back then, we had no cell phones and could not communicate with them after they were disconnected from their aircraft.

Then, quite hesitantly, the four of them turned around and walked back to the bomber, ran-up the engines, and taxied over to the farthermost point on the entire base where they parked the AJ and shut it down after the bombardier reported an atom-bomb warning light emergency only a few moments after the flight-line truck transmitted the same message.

Later, we learned in the debriefing that when the emergency warning light for the atom bomb lit up the cockpit, they all scrambled out and ran for their lives. When their abrupt huddle on the runway was mentioned, they said that essentially they were all winded and had to stop running. Then they decided that if that emergency light was the real deal and that big bad bomb was about to blow up, they realized that they could not run far enough to survive the atomic blast anyway. So they walked back to the AJ with their fingers crossed, each guy saying a lot of private prayers, and undoubtedly promising God that he would mend whatever evil ways were personally involved, which in my friend the third crewman's case, must have been considerable.

Of course, that unscheduled parking place put the control tower within the center of that atom bomb's lethal radius, and we in the control tower were, of course, a bit concerned. Fortunately, the warning light was soon proven to have resulted from a short in the AJ's electrical wiring system (again!) instead of a multi-kiloton atom bomb heating up to cook off and produce another great sink hole in Flaw-rida's fragile ecological system.

15. "ADIOS" ITCHY SOUP STRAINER

Several days later, I was darned glad to be discharged a bit early so that I could play spring football and checkout the mile-high hot tub action at and around Denver University. Just before I left VAH-7 and NAS Sanford for the last time, I made a long-awaited stop at the head (i.e., the bathroom) to finally shave off that itchy darned mustache that I had worn so stubbornly for about six months despite the discomfort, and the unofficial although strongly suggested word passed down from our squadron C.O. in Port Lyautey, French Morocco.

Then, just for the pure heck of it, I made a point of stopping by to show my clean shaven face to the C.O., wave sayonara, and then mambo out the Front Gate to finally return to the real world with my seabag over my shoulder. Losing that darned soup strainer was not a day too soon. I really hated it, but not enough to cave in.

Where I come from, we do something and then we talk about it.

16. SAYONARA SQUADRON VAH-7.

You may have noticed a somewhat less than complementary tone about: (a) the overall tactical concept, but who am I to say anything about that; (b) the extremely iffy primary mission of Navy Squadron VAH-7, but again, who the heck am I to second guess the Pentagon; and (c) our cantankerous, too-soon obsolete AJ-2 Savage bombers in the summer, fall and winter of 1955/1956. What the heck, we had only recently won the prestigious Navy/Marine "E" for "Excellence" award. Of all of the VAH squadrons, VAH-7 was designated the very best heavy attack squadron in the U.S. Navy.

However, within about seven months, VAH-7 subsequently lost two atom bombers: (a) the AJ-2 bomber that slid on its own super slippery hydra lube leakage puddle to fall off the flight deck of the Coral Sea into an anti-aircraft gun tub and be damaged beyond repair; and (b) the AJ-2 bomber whose vertical stabilizer folding mechanism sheared so that its vertical stabilizer continuously smashed against its horizontal stabilizer until that bomber dove inverted into the Sanford City Dump.

Also, we could have lost another AJ-2 bomber and crew if Lt. Millsap had not reacted in a split second to initiate the essential startup procedures for the auxiliary turbojet engine when the whole port radial engine and propeller fell off from the lord mounts forward during the long flight home from Port Lyautey, French Morocco to Sanford, Florida.

The Navy did not need any more chatty reports from me or anyone else. Obviously, the concept of delivering an atom bomb from an already obsolete, poorly performing, undefended, cantankerous airplane was fatally flawed for the updated mission dynamics of 1956. No amount of Herculean effort by the aircrews and maintenance men could ever overcome those impossible hurdles. The new A3D jet bomber was in the pipeline, and we all hoped that it would be an improvement. In some ways it was, but in many ways, it was not.

VI. IN MEMORIUM

The following account of VAH-7's tragic loss of an entire crew is not my sea story because I was no longer with the squadron that following summer of 1956. However, I am making an exception because that fiery crash was such a personal loss to all who knew those brave men. I am not sure, but this tragic accident must have happened during the very last few weeks of Stan (Big Swig) Swigonsky's 20-year (240 months) enlistment as an airborne Navy warrior going back to 1936.

The air battles in the Pacific Theatre from 1941 through 1945 were horrific, and Big Swig was right in the middle of them. He was also standing tall as an aircrew aviator during the Korean War from 1950 to 1953 and the ongoing Cold War.

I don't know the exact date of that fatal accident, but as a rough guess, that could have been Big Swig's last week or possibly his last scheduled flight as an AJ-2 crewman even if that horrendous tragedy had not happened. It had to be within the last week or two of his long-awaited retirement to a newly purchased farm in Pennsylvania after 20 years of outstanding, heroic service to the United States of America. Nobody did it better than Big Swig.

Big Swig, his wife and his children were poised to enjoy the American dream.

I do not have the words to describe how much I admired that guy. He was an inspiration to all of us who knew him, and in so many ways. He was my friend and mentor. I did not look up to very many men in my life, but I looked up to Big Swig. He was my kind of guy.

On the morning of the crash, Lt. Radtke (command pilot), Lt. "Teddy Bear" MacIntosh (bombardier/navigator) and Airman 1st Class Stan "Big Swig" Swigonski (third crewman) were carrying a huge air-to-air refueling tank and dispensing system full of highly combustible JP4 jet fuel in the AJ's bomb bay instead of an inert mockup of the Mark-15 atom bomb. The mission: to practice air-to-air refueling to further that goofy, no-longer-viable subterfuge that VAH-7 was a refueling squadron and not a heavy attack squadron as clearly signified by the squadron's VAH designation for all of the world to see.

Never-mind the large wooden model of "The Navy's Atom Bomber" for anyone to see in downtown Washington D.C. That obsolete subterfuge was apparently a huge waste of time, a waste of money, and the waste of the lives of three very fine U.S. Navy airmen.

After all, we sure as heck were not fooling the Russians or any other potential enemies. I'm sure that they all knew better. Nevertheless, for some unfathomable, hidebound reason known only by the upper layers of the Navy food chain, we were still carrying on with that very dangerous and meaningless subterfuge.

Some months later, I first learned the details about that horrific crash from a member of the NAS Sanford crash crew who had the grizzly job of removing the three badly burned bodies from the wreckage. I met that guy just by random coincidence over a couple of 10-cent beers at the Silver Dollar Bar in Wichita, Kansas when he was also enrolled at Wichita State University in 1957. Then 20 years later, those details were verified by my good friend Frank (Si) Simonsen who was still an AJ-2 air crewman at NAS Sanford at the time of the accident.

According to Si, soon after "wheels up," just as they were beginning to climb out to cruising altitude, one of the two radial engines failed and lost power. Always cool in an emergency, Lt. Radtke nosed over from a climbing to a nose-down gliding flight attitude and called for Lt. MacIntosh to feather that engine's propeller so that they would have a chance to swing around and return to the base. Somehow, Lt. MacIntosh feathered the wrong propeller so that neither engine was providing the thrust needed to keep that aircraft in the air.

No longer able to recover, Si said that Lt. Radtke had only a second or two to pick the crash site. Being the extraordinary man that he was, Lt. Radtke picked a parallel railroad track rather than a school yard. Seconds later that inadequate, too-soon-obsolete bomber crashed in a huge blast of fire and smoke. A split-second later, the entire drop tank full of jet fuel exploded to turn everything—men and airplane—into unrecognizable cinders.

May God have mercy on their souls. As Navy warriors, they did their duty and fought the good fight. They left this earth and their loved ones far too soon. Among many other heroic American warriors, I will always remember them for their staunch dedication and their incredible service to the United States of America.

May they rest in peace,

www.ingramcontent.com/pod-product-compliance
Lightning Source LLC
LaVergne TN
LVHW091548060526
838200LV00036B/748